CLASSROOM
CATALYSTS

CLASSROOM CATALYSTS

15 Efficient Practices That
Accelerate Readers' Learning

Michael F. Opitz
Michael P. Ford

HEINEMANN
Portsmouth, NH

Heinemann

361 Hanover Street

Portsmouth, NH 03801–3912

www.heinemann.com

Offices and agents throughout the world

The authors and publisher wish to thank those who have generously given permission to reprint borrowed material:

Excerpts from the Common Core State Standards © Copyright 2010. National Governors Association Center for Best Practices and Council of Chief State School Officers. All rights reserved.

Appendices A, B, and C: From *Do-able Differentiation: Varying Groups, Texts, and Supports to Reach Readers* by Michael F. Opitz and Michael P. Ford. Copyright © 2008 by Michael F. Opitz and Michael P. Ford. Published by Heinemann, Portsmouth, NH. All rights reserved.

Library of Congress Cataloging-in-Publication Data

Opitz, Michael F.

    Classroom catalysts : 15 efficient practices that accelerate readers' learning / Michael F. Opitz and Michael P. Ford.

        pages   cm

    Includes bibliographical references.

    ISBN 978-0-325-04656-3

    1. Reading comprehension—Study and teaching (Elementary)—Activity programs. 2. Educational acceleration.

I. Ford, Michael P.   II. Title.

LB1573.7.O65 2014

372.47—dc23   2014015576

Editor: Margaret LaRaia

Production: Vicki Kasabian

Cover and interior designs: Suzanne Heiser

Cover images: Shutterstock / Fazakas Mihaly (burst); Shutterstock / pogonici (rainbow paper)

Typesetter: Kim Arney

Manufacturing: Steve Bernier

Printed in the United States of America on acid-free paper

18 17 16 15 14 VP 1 2 3 4 5

CONTENTS

ACKNOWLEDGMENTS

We wish to acknowledge those who helped us create the book you now hold:

- To Kathy Barclay, editor of the Illinois State Reading Journal, who first invited us to put the "many with most" insights and ideas into writing and published our article.
- To previous collaborators Joanne Caldwell and Kathryn Glasswell, whose past work on grouping and text leveling has left a lasting influential effect that shows in this work.
- To colleagues Teri Lesesne, Lori Oczkus, Roland Schendel, Franki Sibberson, Alfred Tatum, and Suzette Youngs, whose work influenced some of the ideas we share in this text.
- To classroom teachers Annette Fitzgerald, Linda Helf, and Greg Kehring, who shared ideas that we used when writing some of the teaching strategies.
- To all those individuals at Heinemann who saw the potential in us and in this book: Kate Montgomery, for showing initial interest; Margaret LaRaia, for editorial support; Vicki Kasabian, for her marvelous editorial production; Eric Chalek, for writing the cover copy and for promoting the book.
- To all, our sincere thanks.

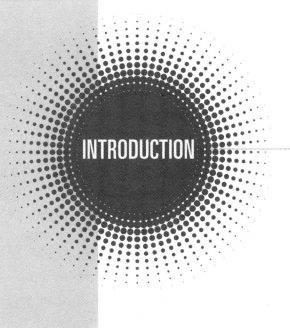

INTRODUCTION

Kids are who they are.

They bring what they bring. They know what they know and we need to stop seeing this as an instructional inconvenience.

P. DAVID PEARSON, "READING POLICY IN AMERICA: A CHECKERED HISTORY, AN UNEASY PRESENT AND AN UNCERTAIN FUTURE"

In his paper "Reading Policy in America," P. David Pearson (2009) reminds us that it would be nice if all the students we teach showed up at the school door primed and ready for formal schooling, but they don't! Students arrive with differences, and expert teaching is about addressing those differences. Gaps between learners are observed at relatively young ages, and many times, those gaps widen as learners move through school experiences. These gaps mean that some students will need to make more than one academic year's worth of growth in an academic year's worth of time. That need surfaces an important question: Are there instructional techniques that provide more bang for the buck and help teachers accelerate students' reading growth? The answer to this question is the focus of this book. But before we turn to how we have written this book to best address this question, we will begin with explaining how we came to see the need for this book. After all, one attribute of effective teachers is that they know why they do what they do.

Understanding the Need for Efficient Practices That Accelerate Readers' Learning

Recently we were both on sabbatical, which gave us the time to visit many classrooms. We saw teachers using best practices and reaching many of their students' reading needs with most of what they needed. They used a variety of texts to engage readers, they met in small groups to target students' reading strengths and needs, and they provided meaningful literacy activities for children who were independently reading and writing away from the teacher. In more than one setting, however, teachers expressed two common frustrations. While they could have been satisfied that they were reaching *many* of their students with *much* of what they needed to grow as readers, they were often frustrated in their efforts to reach *all* of their students with *everything* they needed (Ford and Opitz 2010). Closing the gap between reaching many with much and reaching every with all was a central concern of these teachers. In addition, they expressed frustration that in trying to close that gap, school district personnel usually replaced one approach for teaching reading that reached many of their students with another approach that did more of the same, but fell short of reaching all students, especially those with the greatest reading needs. Listening to their frustrations made us wonder why teachers are rarely encouraged to focus their time and energy on looking at the approaches they are currently using and thinking about what steps they would need to take to make those reading programs work more effectively for more students. Doing so seems a logical place to begin when looking at how to effectively differentiate within central core reading programs, approaches, and frameworks. Could we intensify the instructional reading practices we are currently using—turn up the heat and light, as Bomer (1998) says—to get more bang for our buck? Would this be one way to increase the power of our instruction so that it could accelerate the reading growth of all learners?

After taking a look at dimensions of differentiation in our book *Do-able Differentiation* (2008), we realized that acceleration is the one dimension of differentiation that needs more attention. In essence, acceleration helps teachers focus on getting more bang for their buck. While differentiation implies doing different things for different learners, acceleration implies targeting specific things for specific learners that will cause them to make even greater reading gains. Benjamin Franklin once said, "Never confuse motion with action." In an article called "When Pedagogic Fads Trump Priorities," Mike Schmoker (2010) illustrated the difference to which Franklin was referring when he noted the following:

> [Differentiated instruction] seemed to complicate teachers' work requiring them to procure and assemble multiple sets of materials. I saw frustrated teachers trying to provide materials that matched each student's or group's presumed ability level, interest, preferred modality and learning style. The attempt often devolved into a fanatically assembled collection of worksheets, coloring exercises, and specious kinesthetic activities. And it dumbed down instruction. With so many groups to teach, instructors found it almost impossible to provide sustained, properly executed lessons for each child or group and in a single class period. (22–23)

Schmoker's observation reminds us of the difference between doing something (motion) and doing something that actually makes a positive impact (action). Let's make this distinction a bit more concrete. In the exercise room at a YMCA, we saw a variation on Franklin's words: *Motion is not always action!* In other words, one can spend the same amount of time doing certain exercises that pay off in different ways. Depending on which exercise is chosen and with what intensity the exercise is conducted, one might actually expend more calories in the same amount of time than someone else does with another exercise or with less intensity. The same can be true in instructional settings. Some instructional strategies pay off with greater gains for students who need them.

In trying to reach all students with everything they need, keeping in mind the critical distinction between students' literacy *progress* and students' literacy *proficiency* is also important. The goal of instruction is not just about a learner making progress; it's about a learner becoming proficient. Some current literacy practices have operationalized progress by defining discrete steps that enable teachers to see students making growth. Unfortunately, moving through those small steps often allows teachers to get comfortable with instructional techniques that might be leaving children far short of proficiency. For example, teachers may see growth on timed literacy indicators but lose sight of the fact that by focusing on those indicators, they are not helping the student move forward on more global indicators of reading and writing proficiency. In another instance, teachers might be happy as children advance through two or three levels of a guided reading program but forget the children are still three levels from the benchmark for that grade level. We need to keep our sight on the goal: to help all learners achieve expected proficiencies for each grade level—especially for children who are with us every day, year to year. If our instructional programs can't guarantee proficiency, then the literacy programs, not the students, need to be reexamined.

While acknowledging what others have pointed out about the need to address factors beyond the school walls in our efforts to close these gaps among students (Shannon 2013), in this book we focus on factors within the school walls. Those efforts must be collective efforts because if instruction matters, it matters throughout the school. If instruction is going to lead to accelerated literacy growth for learners with the greatest needs, a schoolwide effort is needed. A significant overarching concern we have after spending time in many classrooms is the amount of variation that exists between one classroom and the next even in the same school building at the same grade level. This variation can happen even when classroom literacy programs share a common core set of materials or common framework (Irvine and Larson 2007). These differences can be both *quantitative* (the amount of instruction students are receiving) and *qualitative* (the substance of instruction students are receiving). Recent research has documented the quantitative variations using teacher logs as a validated means for reporting instructional behaviors (Correnti 2006). In classrooms that Rowan et al. (2009) studied, the variation within a building was often greater than aggregated variations between buildings. Rowan's work found that in some classrooms, students were receiving seventy minutes of literacy instruction a day. In other classrooms, students were receiving 120 minutes of instruction. Imagine the potential impact on student outcomes if some students are receiving fifty more minutes of instruction on a daily basis. It leads to the conclusion that the classroom to which a student is assigned may be the most important variable in explaining a student's outcomes.

Even variations that aren't as obvious can still have a significant impact. Think about two teachers: one who is tight with classroom transitions and another who is a bit loose with the transitions. Let's say that tight transitions save the first teacher ten minutes a day. On any one day that doesn't seem like a lot of time, but if that happens every day over a 180-day school year, it results in an additional 1,800 minutes of instructional time in one school year. That's thirty hours of additional practice. When one teacher chooses to shut down early at the end of the day, end of the week, or end of the year, valuable instructional time is lost, and that has an impact on the students in that classroom.

The amount of time spent teaching is not the only factor that needs to be assessed in guaranteeing standardized opportunities to learn across classrooms. As we saw in the studies on the impact of the Reading First Program (Gamse et al. 2008), teachers did spend more time focused on at least some of the five key elements of reading instruction (phonemic awareness, phonics, fluency, vocabulary, and comprehension) but actually ended up with equal or lower results than in classrooms where less time was spent on the five elements. Therefore, the quality of instruction also matters. Rowan and his team (2006) also documented differences in the quality of literacy instruction from classroom to classroom even *within* schools. Students in some classrooms may spend the majority of their classroom time on relatively low-level content and skills, while their peers in the class next door might be spending much more time on higher-level content.

In our previous work, we have acknowledged the importance of research focused on high-impact exemplary teachers (Pressley et al. 2001; Allington and Johnston 2002). As enlightening as these findings might be, they also suggest that there are teachers who are not high-impact exemplary teachers. Research continues to document this variation. In "Profiles of Educational Quality in First Grade," a study of more than eight hundred first-grade classrooms nationwide, Stuhlman and Pianta (2009) discovered that only 23 percent of first-grade classes were considered of high quality for their academic, social, and emotional climate. An additional 31 percent were socially supportive but of low academic quality, while the rest were rated as either mediocre (28 percent) or of low quality (17 percent). Again, imagine being one of the first graders lucky enough to be placed in a classroom with high-quality academic, social, and emotional climates. Now imagine all the other first graders placed in classrooms with questionable academic, social, or emotional climates. Finally, imagine deciding whether your child will be with a high-impact exemplary teacher or a teacher who is not a high-impact exemplary teacher. Which one would you choose?

Obviously, accelerating the growth of all readers is hard if their opportunities to learn are so varied. Studies like these suggest that if we do not focus on the quality and quantity of instruction the learner receives and instead focus exclusively on the learner, we will continue to fall short in helping to advance the growth of all readers. Perhaps we shouldn't look at how a child is responding to instruction, a cornerstone of response to intervention (RTI), until we've looked at whether all students have had a quality opportunity to learn (OTL).

Applying Research Findings to Develop Fifteen Classroom Catalysts

As Allington and Cunningham (2007) remind us, schools are made up of a collection of classrooms, and classrooms are controlled by individual teachers. In this book, we focus our attention on factors within the control of the individual classroom teacher. We examine the need for intensification in current literacy instructional classroom practices. How do we tighten up, turn up the heat on, or shed more light on what we are doing? How can we get more mileage out of these practices so they reach even more students with more of what they need? We know that some of our learners will need more than an academic year's worth of growth in an academic year's worth of time. They will need what we are identifying as *classroom catalysts* or instructional accelerators—techniques teachers can use to find greater power in their teaching. We start by examining three acceleration principles that move instructional programs closer to reaching every student with all he or she needs:

1. If we want to reach *all* students, we need more effectively designed whole-group lessons.
2. If we want to reach *all* students, we need to make sure small-group work is targeting instructional needs effectively.
3. If we want to reach *all* students, we need to make sure individualized approaches target instructional needs effectively.

We present five practical classroom catalysts for each of these acceleration principles (see Figure I–1). We open each section of the book with a classroom vignette that illustrates the issue and then discuss why the particular

Figure I–1 Acceleration Principles and Classroom Catalysts

Acceleration Principles	Classroom Catalysts
If we want to reach *all* students we need more effectively designed whole-group lessons.	• name cards • class lists • interactive guides • structured listening guides • directed listening-thinking activities (DLTAs)
If we want to reach *all* students, we need to make sure small-group work is targeting instructional needs effectively.	• discussion matrices • small-group taping and analysis • warm-up cards • picture walk alternatives • word count boosters
If we want to reach *all* students, we need to make sure individualized approaches target instructional needs effectively.	• silent reading assessments • text selection guidelines for silent reading • stamina-building activities • reading out loud with partners • text response activities

recommendation is important. We then present five corresponding classroom catalysts and answer five questions to explain each of them:

1. What is the goal?
2. Why is the goal important?
3. How can you evaluate your current efforts in meeting this goal?
4. What can you use to make progress in meeting this goal?
5. How else can you use this technique to accelerate instruction?

We embed a brief research base and ideas for adaptation when addressing these questions. We also close the discussion of each catalyst with a classroom vignette that shows a teacher using the given accelerator to address the issue highlighted at the beginning of the section.

Taken together, the ideas we present herein accelerate instruction by

- fully believing that all students can achieve and designing instruction that sets students up for success so that they do achieve relative to the stated objectives of the lesson.
- using what students know to teach them something they need to know. Students are seen as half full rather than half empty.
- helping teachers use time more efficiently, reserving the extra saved minutes for instruction and learning.
- providing students with scaffolded instruction as they tackle complex texts with a vocabulary and content that might be considered beyond their reach.
- keeping students engaged the entire instructional time (i.e., time on task) which makes heightened learning more likely because students minds are totally present.
- holding high expectations for all learners and designing instruction that will enable all students to meet these expectations.
- capitalizing on one or more of five motivation generalizations to engage students. As summarized by Pintrich (2003) and adapted by Opitz and Ford (2014), the five generalizations that motivate students are as follows:
  1. Adaptive self-efficacy and competence beliefs.
  2. Adaptive attributions and control beliefs.
  3. Higher levels of interest and intrinsic motivation.
  4. Higher levels of value.
  5. Setting and attaining goals.

In other words, you accelerate learning when you maximize expectations, target instruction, use your time wisely, and offer support.

✳   ✳   ✳

Our goal with this book is to shift the focus of conversations from discussions of how to reach many students with most of what they need to how to reach *every* with *all*. Our aim is to heighten awareness of the acceleration dimension of differentiated reading instruction and offer this book as a catalyst for this awareness and ensuing discussions about differentiation. We hope that as a result of examining and reflecting on the contents within these pages, readers will see that they may have to rethink assumptions behind some critical institutionalized ideas, but nothing should be sacred or off the table. Serving students rather than orthodoxies or programs is a sure way to accelerate literacy instruction and student growth.

Intensifying
Whole-Group
Instruction

Research on classroom discourse

illustrates that the activities that constitute whole-class instruction are not inherently problematic for low-achieving students and can, in fact, promote engagement.

SEAN KELLY AND JULIANNE TURNER, "RETHINKING THE EFFECTS OF CLASSROOM ACTIVITY STRUCTURE ON THE ENGAGEMENT OF LOW-ACHIEVING STUDENTS"

elle has prepared an enlarged big-book text on habitats from her science unit that she will use during a shared reading experience. While she has many texts for her reading/language arts block, her science program has only one text for all students. As the students return from recess, she invites them to sit on the carpet in front of the big-book easel. She waits for all students to find their way to the carpet and then settles down her group. She begins to explore the cover of the book, asking her students what they think the word *habitat* means and what they know about habitats. She quickly calls on Matt and Michelle, whose hands go up first, and they take over the discussion, almost exclusively responding to all of Elle's questions. At one point, Elle surveys the group and sees that many have moved to the edge of the carpet and have lost eye contact. She asks all to look at her to regain their attention but then finds Matt and Michelle resuming the discussion. By the end of the reading, many of the kids seem to have little to contribute to extend the discussion. She closes the book and kids rush back to their desks and other spaces in the room to engage in other activities. She wonders if anyone has gained anything from the discussion of the text. Matt and Michelle seemed to already know the content, and most of the other kids seemed very disengaged. Elle is left feeling frustrated by the results of the large-group lesson. She has used big books before and students have seemed engaged. She wonders what went wrong today and how she can prevent this from happening in the future.

Why Is It Important to Strengthen Whole-Group Instruction?

As much as classroom teachers have experimented with and implemented structures to facilitate small-group and individualized reading and writing components, students still spend a significant amount of time in whole-class settings. Kelly and Turner (2009) reported that students of all grades (i.e., first through twelfth) may spend up to two hours a day in whole-class settings. In some ways, that makes sense. For providing universal instruction to all students, the whole-class setting is the most efficient in terms of time and resources. If there is something teachers can teach to all their students, they should use the whole-class setting. It keeps all students together to minimize the amount of time needed for instruction and allows for the use of one set of materials for all learners. If teachers are going to accelerate the growth of all learners, however, they need to be careful about overusing whole-class instruction, especially when the purpose is something other than providing the same instruction to all learners. Teachers must also know when to move toward the use of targeted small-group instruction and individualized instruction in working with students to have the maximum impact.

The first and perhaps most important dimension that needs to be examined during whole-class lessons is the overall level of student engagement. The only way large-group lessons benefit learners is if the learners stay engaged during those lessons. We want as many learners to get as much as possible out of the universal instruction provided in the large group. By intentionally addressing issues like overall levels of engagement during whole-class instruction, teachers may actually reduce demands on other components of the literacy program to accelerate the growth of all learners.

But how do you know if learners are engaged? Wlodkowski and Ginsberg (1995) defined engagement as the visible outcome of motivation, the natural capacity to direct energy in the pursuit of a goal. It usually happens when learners can sense success is within their reach, they value the outcome of the learning experience, and they feel safe in the classroom setting (Brophy 1987). During a whole-group lesson, then, a teacher would look for attentive students who are focused on completing a given task and persist even if the task becomes difficult because they are valuing what they are doing and deriving meaning from it. One sure way to double-check these observations is to talk with students as they complete their work and listen to what they have to say about it: Comments such as "I am having trouble understanding this section but I really want to know about how gravity works. I think I need to look at more of the diagrams to help me understand" are indicative of engaged students.

The importance of student engagement cannot be overstated. The ability to generate high levels of engagement is one characteristic of high-impact exemplary teachers (Pressley et al. 2001). In classrooms where teachers had a greater impact on performance and achievement measures, engagement levels were as high as 90/90—that is, 90 percent of the students were engaged 90 percent of the time. In classrooms of exemplary teachers who had less impact on performance and achievement measures, engagement levels were around 60/60 (60 percent of the students were engaged 60 percent of the time).

One way to move closer to reaching every student with all that he or she needs in large-group settings, then, is to focus on engagement levels. Assessing baseline levels of student engagement leads to improving on them as needed. One way to improve is to explore techniques that keep more learners engaged during whole-group lessons.

Although whole-group lessons can be problematic when trying to differentiate instruction, they can be created by using models that are more conducive to differentiation. We have discussed models that work with different levels of readers when using one common text (Caldwell and Ford 2002; Opitz and Ford 2008). Paratore (1990) described one model as grouping without tracking (see Appendix A for tips on planning a grouping-without-tracking lesson). In this model, teachers use groups to vary levels of support during the reading and the response to a whole-class text. Those students who can read and respond to the text on their own are guided indirectly while the teacher guides those students who need support to read and respond to the text more directly. This model addresses acceleration by providing high expectations for all readers with the same quality of meaning-based instruction but with variable levels of support. By varying levels of support, the model avoids dumbing down materials, instruction, or expectations for some readers, especially those who need the most help. It provides respectful work for all learners—work that all learners see as valuable (Tomlinson 1999).

This model also addresses acceleration by providing mediated, scaffolded instruction (i.e., gradual release). The gradual release of responsibility guarantees that no learner starts the reading of the more complex whole-class text cold (Frey, Fisher, and Everlove 2009). The teacher makes sure the lesson begins with some sort of warm-up, such as a read-aloud, think-aloud, or write-aloud that models what the learners will need to do with their own reading. It also enables learners to get the first chunk of the text in their heads through the teacher's modeling of it. The teacher then invites the students in on the next chunk of the text using choral readings and prompting group thinking during interactive writing. Finally, the teacher steps back a bit and monitors the students as they work together on the next chunk of reading, thinking, and writing together. This three-step process builds a firm foundation for all learners to move toward more independent work with the text. It should be noted that while the gradual release of responsibility is recommended as a way of designing strategy instruction, a recent study (DeWitz, Jones, and Leahy 2009) revealed that rarely do core programs follow the gradual release-of-responsibility model.

Another whole-class model that can improve the design of whole-class instruction is jigsawing (see Appendix B). First proposed by Aronson (1978), this is a model we have discussed in our previous work (Opitz and Ford 2002; Opitz and Ford 2008). With jigsawing, there is one text for the whole class, but the text has the possibility of being divided into different parts for different groups of readers. This allows for a better match of text demands to readers. Teachers can divide up the text, match groups of learners to appropriate parts of the text, and then vary their levels of support by providing more direct support to groups that might need it and providing indirect support to other groups that can operate more independently. One significant advantage of the jigsaw model is that it allows all learners to share power in making contributions to the large group. Since no group has read the entire text, it allows all groups to bring something different to the class discussion. This is another way to keep all learners engaged and move closer to reaching every reader with all that he or she needs.

Although we offer these ways to engage all students within whole-class instruction, we recognize that many teachers may have concerns. The use of whole-class instruction has been somewhat controversial because in the past many students were assigned difficult texts with very little instructional support, spending most of their classroom time with texts they couldn't read. Many schools responded to this overuse of whole-class texts by moving to the use of small-group models like guided reading that included use of at-level texts usually with lots of support. But in their study of fluency-oriented reading instruction (FORI), Stahl and Heubach (2005) discovered that when students were given more challenging whole-class texts accompanied by scaffolded instruction by the teacher, they made greater gains than those students who only spent time working with at-level texts or challenging texts without support. These findings are in keeping with what we advocate here: properly supporting readers with more challenging texts can accelerate their progress. One main ingredient is teacher support with an eye on student independence.

The use of more complex texts may get even more attention as career and college readiness standards are launched by more states. Look at this college and career readiness standard from the Common Core State Standards (NGA Center for Best Practices and CCSSO 2010): "Read and comprehend complex literary and informational texts independently and proficiently" (ELA-Literacy.CCRA.R.10). At specific grade levels, the related standards recommend spending time with complex texts. For example, in grade 2: "By the end of the year, read and comprehend literature . . . in the grades 2–3 text complexity band proficiently with scaffolding as needed at the high end of the range" (ELA-Literacy.RL.2.10). In grade 3: "By the end of the year, read and comprehend literature . . . at the high end of the grades 2–3 text complexity band independently and proficiently" (ELA-Literacy.RL.3.10). This language is repeated at other levels as well. Look at the fourth- and fifth-grade language: "By the end of the year, read and comprehend literature . . . in the grades 4–5 text complexity band proficiently, with scaffolding as needed at the high end of the range" (ELA-Literacy.RL.4.10) and "By the end of the year, read and comprehend literature . . . at the high end of the grades 4–5 text complexity band independently and proficiently" (ELA-Literacy.RL.5.10). As the International Reading Association reminds teachers, "guidelines on text complexity encourage teachers to engage students in reading at least some texts they are likely to struggle with in terms of fluency and comprehension" (2012, 1). Clearly, if teachers are to use such texts with maximum results, they will need instructional resources and ideas for supporting learners.

Five Classroom Catalysts for Intensifying Whole-Group Instruction

Beyond the models we discussed previously, we present five classroom catalysts for accelerating the growth of all learners in addressing key issues within whole-group instruction:

1. Name cards
2. Class lists

3. Interactive guides

4. Structured listening guides

5. Directed listening-thinking activities

We start with name cards, which may seem a bit mechanical but are a very concrete teacher-directed way to raise the engagement levels of all learners, especially those who often disengage most frequently. They are a good starting point and can be a useful management tool. Class lists are a more subtle way to capture the engagement levels in large groups and serve as another tool to enhance calling on students systematically. Interactive guides provide a whole-group tool by which the teacher can guide hands-on participation in a large group, improving engagement, encouraging processing, and assisting overall learning as the students take more responsibility for their learning. Structured listening guides are built to guide the teacher to open up even more spaces for students to listen and learn. They provide opportunities for learners to take more responsibility for learning as they improve their listening abilities. Finally, directed listening-thinking activities help students internalize a process and structure for learning in whole groups that they can transfer to different contexts and contents.

Each of the classroom catalysts is illustrated with classroom examples and/or appropriate support materials and each is framed around five questions:

1. What is my goal?

2. Why is the goal important?

3. How can I evaluate my current efforts in meeting this goal?

4. What can I use to make progress in meeting this goal?

5. How else can I use this technique to accelerate instruction?

Although each of these ideas can stand alone, more powerful instruction can emerge when you see the connections among them. They are designed to help you move from more teacher-directed to teacher-guided whole-group techniques where students are asked to take increasing responsibility for their levels of engagement, listening abilities, and ultimately their own learning. Look at the ideas as interrelated tools to tighten up your whole-group instruction to accelerate the growth of all learners. Instructional acceleration begins with the teacher having tools to capture, analyze, and improve the levels of engagement of students in the large-group instructional setting. Instructional acceleration occurs when the teacher uses techniques like these and eventually transfers the responsibility to the students to operate effectively by themselves.

Name Cards

What Is the Goal?

To accelerate the growth of all readers in whole-group settings, maintaining high levels of engagement is critical. Teachers must assess where their students' baseline levels of engagement are and then structure their whole-class instruction to raise engagement levels to rival those of high-impact exemplary teachers—90 percent of their students on task 90 percent of the time.

Why Is the Goal Important?

Children spend significant amounts of instructional time in large-group settings. We know that the universal instruction provided in whole-class lessons is still the most efficient use of teaching time and resources. Whole-group instruction allows us to address all learners using minimal resources at the same time. The challenge of whole-group instruction is maintaining levels of engagement across diverse learners.

Some children learn quite early that it is very easy to disengage in large-group settings and let others assume responsibility for responding to the teacher. Many students quickly learn to move to the edge of the carpet during large-group lessons and keep their heads down, hoping that the teacher will call on other students who always seem to be ready to volunteer. Unfortunately, the power of whole-class instruction erodes when those who need the instruction the most have learned to disengage from it.

We also know that overreliance on a language interaction pattern labeled I-R-E promotes disengagement in large-group settings. The teacher *initiates* a question. Usually a single student *responds* with a short or one-word answer, and then the teacher *evaluates* the answer with a global, generic comment (e.g., "Good answer."). This language interaction creates a passive environment in which one or a few learners respond while most observe. Breaking this pattern and replacing it with one that will invite more students into the conversation is necessary to accelerate the growth of all students.

How Can You Evaluate Your Current Efforts in Meeting This Goal?

While you might think you can intuitively monitor your levels of interaction in whole-group settings, you could probably do that more effectively and realistically if you used a second pair of eyes or ears. If you have the possibility of working with a resource person, that person could become your second pair of eyes and ears; however, when that is not possible, you can take a second look by taping one of your large-group lessons. An audiotape might be the easiest way to start, but the increasing convenience of digital video recording devices may allow you to just as easily capture the lesson visually as well. Using the Whole-Group Engagement Analysis Form (see Figure 1–1), you can analyze students' current engagement levels. Just knowing that you are recording your interactions may raise your awareness to a more conscious level, preventing you from falling into traditional interaction patterns. Use the form again after implementing the name cards to see whether you have improved in your effort to raise engagement levels in whole-class lessons.

What Can You Use to Make Progress in Meeting This Goal?

You can create name cards to help you more systematically call on students to increase the number of students involved in interaction and reduce the number of students disengaged during the whole-class setting. You could use the template included in Figure 1–2 or index cards of a similar size. Make one card for each student. Write the student's first name on the front of the card and the student's last name on the back. Make sure the name is written clearly in dark letters and is large enough to be read from a distance.

Whenever you move to the large-group setting, keep the name cards close at hand. Tell students that instead of raising their hands to participate, they should watch for their names to come up on the cards. You can start by saying the name on the first card, but sometimes you can just flash the card without saying anything to help all eyes stay focused on you. Instead of responding to the child's answer, systematically ask the next student in the stack of cards to judge the response ("What do you think about that answer?"). This also allows you to provide language models for how to extend a previous student response. If it looks like students are disengaging once their cards have been pulled, let them see you file those cards back in the middle of the stack so they know they might be called on again. Another way to keep students engaged is to ask a question, wait for a show of hands for those who want to answer, and then draw a name card. The student whose name is on the card is the one who gets to provide the answer.

Beyond keeping students engaged, which makes heightened learning more likely, using name cards is a way to accelerate younger students' learning about print features such as how capital letters are used to signal first and last names, the letters that are used to spell different names, and the sounds associated with those letters. So, by using name cards, students get additional, meaningful learning opportunities to develop and use features of print. As a result, less instructional time is needed to develop these skills.

How Else Can You Use This Technique to Accelerate Instruction?

You can use name cards to intensify instruction in four other ways.

1. To convene students in a meeting area or to dismiss them from that meeting area.
2. To quickly pair up students or form small groups.
3. To randomly assign students to classroom tasks.
4. To provide students with word activities. Place the cards at a word work station when you're not using them so students can sort the names by length, by letter patterns, or by sounds.

The first three ways accelerate instruction by saving class time that can then be used to focus students on specific content they need to learn. The fourth idea accelerates instruction by giving students meaningful words to use for sorting activities that reinforce their understandings of print. Therefore, less time will be needed for direct instruction related to these print concepts and can be used instead to teach other content students need to learn.

having reflected on her disappointing shared book lesson, Elle has prepared a follow-up shared reading text on habitats from her science unit. But this time, she has decided to use name cards to engage more of her students. She grabs her name cards and moves to her seat by the carpet. She asks the students to watch for their names and uses the cards to move her children from their desks to the carpet. As she flashes the cards, she also pairs students up and asks them to sit with their study buddies on the carpet, making sure that they each bring a pencil and a clipboard holding a simple note-taking guide that she has prepared ahead of time.

Once all are seated, she explores the new text, then asks an open-ended question that invites answers that the students can confirm as they share the text. She reminds students to think about the answers in their heads first. She consciously ticks off three seconds of wait time before moving to a new direction or asking for a response. She invites partners to turn, talk, and listen as they share their answers with each other and then record possible answers as best as they can on their note-taking guides.

Once students have had ample time to talk, she flashes a name card and asks that student and his or her partner to share their answer. She flashes a second card and asks that student's team to respond to the first team's answer. As she reads the text, she invites the teams to listen and see if they can confirm their responses. She suggests a choral signal such as a clap to indicate if the team was on track with its response. She elicits student responses three more times as they explore the whole-class text.

Once the class has finished exploring the book, she uses her name cards to dismiss each student. They exit the carpet by sharing one thing they have learned or a new question they might have. She asks them to leave their clipboards behind, and when she has a free minute, she quickly looks through the students' note-taking guides to see which partners seem to have been engaged and on target, using their written comments as evidence. Her review leaves her feeling successful in that their comments show that almost all the kids have gained something from the discussion. Elle walks back to her desk, encouraged by the results of the large-group lesson and reflecting on how she can make it even tighter the next time.

Figure 1–1 Whole-Group Engagement Analysis Form

Whole-Group Engagement Analysis Form

Directions: Record two or more whole-group lessons of similar duration and content over time. Replay the recordings and analyze the following elements for each lesson. If the list appears too unwieldy, choose those that you most want to know about and save the others for another time. Reflect on instructional techniques that led to improvement and additional steps to take in continuing your growth.

	Whole-Group Lesson Baseline Analysis	Whole-Group Lesson Subsequent Analysis	Reflection on Differences
Number of Students Involved in Interaction			
Number of Questions Asked			
Number of Closed Questions (i.e., questions that require a one-word or short answer and are often directly stated within a text)			
Number of Open-Ended Questions (i.e., questions that call on learners to provide longer answers using stated and unstated information to derive an answer)			
Wait Time After Each Question			
Invitations for Choral/ Whole-Class Unison Responses			
Invitations to Talk with Partners			
Teacher Use of One-Word Praise			

Figure 1–1 *Continued*

Whole-Group Engagement Analysis Form

	Whole-Group Lesson Baseline Analysis	Whole-Group Lesson Subsequent Analysis	Reflection on Differences
Teacher Use of Specific Praise			
Number of Probing Follow-Up Questions			
Teacher Probing of Accuracy (Questioning Only to Get Right Answer)			
Teacher Probing of Problem Solving (Questioning the How and Why Behind Answers)			
Number of Prompting Questions (i.e., How and why follow-up questions used to lead students to explain their thinking processes and answers)			
Efforts to Systematically Call on Students			
Number of Students Off Task			
Other Noticeable Engagement Factors			

Figure 1–2 Name Cards

Name Cards

Class Lists

What Is the Goal?

As you work on raising the level of engagement in whole-class instruction to that 90/90 level, strive to reach that level with less teacher control. You want to see as many students as possible feel comfortable, confident, and competent enough to make important contributions on their own during large-group instruction.

Why Is the Goal Important?

Using name cards as a way to raise levels of engagement in whole-group instruction means that engagement levels are derived from teacher-control mechanisms. To see if students' participation rates will remain high without those teacher controls, you'll need to attempt less teacher-directed management of your large-group instruction. That will also allow you to temporarily retire the name cards teaching technique before it is worn out. You can always grab the name cards when the teaching moment warrants it, but you want to avoid overusing them.

How Can You Evaluate Your Current Efforts in Meeting This Goal?

While you can continue to use the techniques previously described in the Whole-Group Engagement Analysis Form (Figure 1–1) to evaluate student attentiveness, you can also use a simpler, quicker tool to judge engagement during whole-group instruction: a class list. Create a class list by putting the names of your students down the left side of a grid and building columns for informally coding large-group responses during different large-group instructional activities. To determine a baseline level of interaction, simply use a plus-or-minus coding system. As a student makes a positive contribution during the activity, place a plus sign (+) next to the student's name. If a student makes a questionable contribution during the activity, code it with a minus sign (–). At the end of the activity, you will be able to analyze not only the frequency of students' responses but also the general quality of those responses. If you are lucky enough to have collaborators, you can trade off recording these data as you take turns teaching.

What Can You Use to Make Progress in Meeting This Goal?

As with the name cards, class lists help accelerate instruction by ensuring that all students get to participate in a whole class lesson, providing more equalized opportunities to learn. Instead of students passively sitting and letting others respond, teachers can use the list as a way of noting who is and is not participating by glancing at the markings on the list. They can then draw out those students who have been responding less frequently than their peers.

Additionally, class lists allow teachers to capture data that often go unrecorded. By noting the number and quality of responses made collectively by the group and individually by students, teachers can use that information to inform their thinking as they plan for more strategic whole-class instruction in subsequent lessons.

Get your students used to the fact that whenever you are working in the large group, they will see you holding your clipboard and making some marks while you work together. After getting a sense of the baseline of students' participation in whole-group activities, you can use the class list to help you more systematically call on students. Although in your head and heart you might think you are calling on all students as you work in whole groups, a formal record of the flow of a large-group interaction might show that certain students participate more frequently than others. If so, try to be more intentional in balancing participation. Because the class list shows who has contributed, you can make sure to call on those whose voices you haven't heard. As you move into the large group, you can highlight three or four students you want to call on first to get their voices heard, instead of relying on the regular self-initiators (Ford 2005).

How Else Can You Use This Technique to Accelerate Instruction?

Try to keep your clipboard with you at all times. Instead of filing anecdotal information away in your head or heart, keep track of critical data that emerge in your classroom all day long on the class list. For example, you can capture miscues during short oral readings, leading to teachable moments at an appropriate time either with the whole class or with an individual student. You can record a spelling attempt a student makes during a whole-class lesson and determine whether to discuss the spelling attempt when conferencing with that student. You can introduce the class list as a record-keeping tool for the students to use in keeping track of daily tasks. Finally, you can make clipboards with class lists readily available for students to use in collecting their own data as their friends respond to survey questions as a part of a larger lesson (e.g., a mathematics graphing lesson that focuses on students' favorite colors, number of people in their households, pets, and so on).

elle retires her name cards for the next lesson in the habitat unit. Before it starts, Elle reminds her students that just like they have been using their clipboards to take notes, she is going to use her clipboard to do the same. She is going to study her teaching and what all are learning when they work in the large group. She shows them her clipboard, which contains a prepared class list form. She invites the students to make their way to the large-group meeting area by asking them to watch her and walk over when she makes eye contact. Elle quickly moves down her list, silently making eye contact to transition her students one by one to the meeting area. She prepares the group for an interactive reading of a common text focused on desert habitats. As she taps background knowledge with prepared open-ended questions, she watches to see which learners are confident and comfortable enough to respond. She records plus signs by the names of individual students as they respond with appropriate answers and minus signs by names of students who give inappropriate answers. As she moves into the text, she stops at planned pages to help learners process the information. She switches to a different-color pen. She checks her class list and calls on students who have not contributed yet to the discussion. She records their responses with the same simple coding system. At the end of the lesson, she dismisses her students from the area one by one as they identify one important thing they have learned about deserts. She starts with those who have not voluntarily contributed to the discussion yet. She asks the first third of the group to use quiet voices and whisper their important things to her as they leave the carpet. That leaves the possibility of the middle third responding with their own answers—not just repeating others they've heard—before she calls on those who she knows will be able to add to the growing list of insights and ideas revealed verbally and nonverbally. After the lesson, Elle looks at the data on her class list and sees that she was able to hear from every learner at least once. She is starting to see a pattern that highlights who her voluntary responders are and whom she needs to be more intentional about drawing into the large-group discussions.

Interactive Guides

What Is the Goal?

Using name cards and class lists should allow you to really become more intentional about honoring the voices of all your students in the large-group setting. Now you can strive to make sure your instruction in large groups assists all students in processing, remembering, and transferring the information being shared.

Why Is the Goal Important?

Your large-group instruction provides you the most efficient use of time and energy. You have all your students in one place at one time and can use one text to support your instruction. It provides a critical opportunity for initial universal instruction. You want to seize this opportunity to maximize the learning of as many students as possible so that you can minimize your need to repeat the lesson or provide follow-up instruction to individuals. The time that you would normally use to repeat lessons can then be used to teach additional content, thus accelerating instruction. Maximizing learning depends on student engagement but also on supporting the instruction so that it shifts students from a more passive form of listening to a more active form. You also want to help your students begin to internalize ways of comprehending texts. Through your shared work, you can guide them to use processes such as activating prior knowledge, monitoring understanding, and determining importance as they work with class texts. Through whole-group lessons, you can model how they can understand texts when reading independently.

How Can You Evaluate Your Current Efforts in Meeting This Goal?

You can easily set up a before-and-after situation to judge how well your students can process, remember, and transfer information from an interactive read-aloud or shared reading. Select two texts of comparable content and level to share with them. Share the first text without the use of a processing guide. Plan to use the same prompts you would use with an interactive guide, but keep the discussion in an oral mode. The next day, start your lesson by asking the learners to each fold a piece of paper into four boxes. In three boxes, ask them to write or draw important things they should remember from what they learned from the text you read the previous day. Ask them to circle the one idea they think is the most important. In the fourth box, using a three-point scale with 1 being "not well" and 3 meaning "very well," ask them to rate how well they remembered the information from the day before. Collect their sheets and analyze how well the students processed and remembered the information without the use of an interactive guide. Repeat the same process using the second text with an interactive guide. On the next day, you can see the level of information they processed and remembered. Comparing the data from the two activities will let you see if the interactive guide helped maximize the learning for as many students as possible. You can gradually de-emphasize the direct use of interactive guides to see if their use over time has helped your students internalize ways of comprehending texts.

What Can You Use to Make Progress in Meeting This Goal?

Interactive guides are simple graphic organizers you can develop to guide the listening or viewing of your students in large-group settings. Look closely at the text you are going to use for an interactive reading with the whole group. Strategically look for six key stopping points along the way. You will ask your learners to stop and process what is happening in the text at those moments. Intentionally decide what you are going to ask the students at those stopping points and put little notes reminding yourself where to stop and what to ask about the text (Figure 1–3). Develop an interactive guide with six numbered boxes on a sheet of paper, or use the template provided in Figure 1–4. Prepare a copy for each student. To make it easier to work with the materials, you might have the students stay at their tables while you move around the room with the book. Start with a question to activate prior knowledge based on the work you have already done with the topic. Invite the students to draw and/or write something they already know about the topic in the first box on their interactive guide. When finished, the students can talk at their tables about what they have learned so far and you can drop in on their conversations. Then read aloud the book to the first stopping point. Pause briefly and ask the learners what is one important thing they should remember from what you have read so far. Ask them to note that in the second box on their interactive guide. After table conversations, continue to share the next portion of the book. Pause briefly again and ask the students what they should remember from this part of the book. They should note this in the third box on their interactive guide. Talk briefly about what they have learned from this part and keep reading until the end of the book. Invite the students to use the fourth box to record one more thing they want to remember from the book. Talk about all the things they want to remember. If the book is relatively short, consider rereading it. Focus their attention on listening carefully for one more thing they want to remember. When you finish, ask them to record that idea in the fifth box. After the second reading, make a chart of the important things they want to remember. Then guide your students to see what the main idea for the book is. Before you finish the lesson, ask all the students to rate how well they worked in the large group on a scale of 1 to 3: a 3 means they worked the best they possibly could, a 2 means they worked pretty well but could improve, and a 1 means they did OK but need to try harder next time. Have them add their ratings to the last box on the interactive guide.

In what way does this use of an interactive guide accelerate instruction? All students are held to the same high expectation—that they will participate and can complete the activity. This mindset and scaffolded way of helping students complete the guide provides students with a meaningful way to use what they know about literacy (especially listening, speaking, reading, and writing). This added practice helps accelerate their learning because they are actually applying what they are learning. Application is a higher-level mental process that enables learning to have staying power.

How Else Can You Use This Technique to Accelerate Instruction?

Interactive guides can be developed in many different ways to focus learners on different ways of thinking about and responding to shared texts. As the example read-aloud plan in Figure 1–5 shows, you can look closely at the text on each page of a book and then plan an appropriate prompt. Some of the prompts can include some word-level clues. Remember, even if some readers might struggle with the word choices, you can clearly pronounce the options before students make their choices. Once you have developed the prompts, you can quickly set up the interactive guide in a manner that supports learning from this specific text (see Figure 1–6).

As shown in the examples presented, interactive guides can be developed to focus on word-level strategies ("Can you use your strategies to figure out this word and draw a picture of it in your box?"), word-meaning strategies ("Can you predict a word that would make sense here? Write or draw that word in your box"), or comprehension strategies ("Write in the box the most important event so far"). Once you have introduced the tool and used it in large groups with familiarity, you can modify it for use to guide readers in small groups or independently. The same techniques can be used for tightening up the learners' viewing skills and listening skills for other modes besides print-based activities (e.g., guest speakers or oral reports).

All of these alternative ways provide opportunities for students to apply known skills in meaningful ways without a lot of direct instruction. In this way, they accelerate students' literacy growth because they call on students to use higher-level thinking skills to complete literacy tasks, and higher-level learning produces learning with staying power. Less time spent reviewing content allows more time for learning new content, which thereby increases students' knowledge base. They also provide a sense of ownership, which enables students to stay motivated and engaged. The interactive guides provide a "paper trail" documenting the level of engagement and understanding of each student. By collecting and quickly reviewing these, teachers can more effectively target follow-up instruction and adjust instruction in future whole-group settings.

elle selects the book *Changing Seasons* (Greydanus 1983) from the Now I Know series for her interactive read-aloud. She previews the book and decides to present half of the book to her students in a large-group setting. She decides to intensify the students' engagement with the text as she reads it. Instead of using her name cards or class list to monitor the large-group instruction, she prepares an interactive guide for each student. She selects nine prompts and writes each on a sticky note to place on the pages as reminders of what she wants her students to think about (see Figure 1–5). She distributes the interactive guides and invites her students to stay at their tables today while she displays the pages of the book as she moves around the room. She stops for each prompt and provides time for her students to respond. When she hits the halfway point of the book, she decides to let the students check their answers. She brings out multiple smaller copies of the big book. She hands individual copies to a couple of her stronger readers who she knows will be able to reread on their own and check their answers. She pairs up a few other students to work together to check their answers with a copy of the book, and she gathers a small group of students in need of more support to work through the text a second time. When all the students have had a chance to look at their answers, she gathers them back together in a large group to discuss what they have learned.

Figure 1–3 Interactive Guide Planning Form

Interactive Guide Planning Form

Title of Interactive Read-Aloud	
Prior Knowledge Prompt for Box 1	
Stop-and-Process Prompt for Box 2	
Stop-and-Process Prompt for Box 3	
Stop-and-Process Prompt for Box 4	
Rereading Prompt for Box 5	
Self-Evaluation Prompt for Box 6	

Figure 1–4 Interactive Guide

Interactive Guide

1.	**2.**
3.	**4.**
5.	**6.**

Figure 1–5 Sample Interactive Read-Aloud

Text: *Changing Seasons*	Prompt
Page 1: Look at the pretty flower.	**Read aloud.**
Page 2: There are new plants growing in the ground.	**Read aloud.**
Page 3: It is spring!	**Box 1: Have students predict what season it is based on clues (cover up the word *spring*).**
Page 4: The trees are covered with fat buds.	**Box 2: Have students look at picture and guess what the trees are covered with (cover up the word *buds*).**
Page 5: Inside, tiny leaves are growing.	**Box 3: Have the students write or draw what are growing inside the green things (cover up the word *leaves*).**
Page 6: The animals are busy making new homes.	**Box 4: Have the students write or draw what the animals are busy making (cover up the word *homes*).**
Page 7: They are busy taking care of their new babies, too!	**Box 5: Have the students write or draw what the animals are taking care of (cover up the word *babies*).**
Page 8: In spring, each day grows a little longer.	**Box 6: Give students a choice between *longer* and *shorter* (cover up the word *longer*).**
Page 9: The sun is a little higher in the sky.	**Box 7: Give students a choice between *lower* and *higher* (cover up the word *higher*).**
Page 10: So, each day grows warmer and warmer.	**Box 8: Give students a choice between *colder* and *warmer* (cover up the word *warmer*).**
Page 11: Soon it is summer!	**Box 9: Have students predict what season it will be next (cover up the word *summer*).**

Figure 1–6 Sample Interactive Read-Aloud Guide

Name:	1.
2.	3.
4.	5.
6. **longer** **shorter**	7. **lower** **higher**
8. **colder** **warmer**	9.

Structured Listening Guides

What Is the Goal?

The goal is to use whole-group instruction to engage your students in learning how to listen and how to use listening better to learn. You can use name cards, class lists, and interactive guides to raise levels of engagement for your students during whole-group instruction. Ultimately you want your students to learn to be better listeners without these teacher supports. You want them to learn that they can use listening strategies to think more deeply about information they are receiving from orally delivered sources. For example, you want *all* students to know how to use listening to make inferences about what they are hearing (how to listen "between the lines") so they can build a foundation for making inferences as they read.

Why Is the Goal Important?

Much of the information your students will receive will come from oral sources rather than written sources. While you might be very intentional about teaching students to handle written text, you might realize that you have been less intentional about teaching them to learn from what they have heard. Expecting students to listen is far different from teaching them how. You want to make sure that all students understand that listening happens more inside the head rather than outside of it. Teaching students how to listen improves their listening comprehension, which in turn improves their reading comprehension (see Opitz and Zbaracki 2004). And as experts have noted (Alvermann 1984), this is especially true if (a) the listening skills relate to reading (e.g., making inferences), (b) students are actively involved in related extension activities, and (c) various forms of literature are used. Capitalizing on developing students' listening comprehension is an excellent way to accelerate their reading comprehension because they can use the same skills they acquired through listening when reading; they already have a mindset for what these comprehension skills are.

How Can You Evaluate Your Current Efforts in Meeting This Goal?

One way to teach students how to listen is to use a structured listening guide. Using the structured listening guide, you can teach students how to listen to see if the source is providing all requisite information or expecting that they will fill in necessary information so that they can understand the intended message. Some experts have suggested using a structured listening guide as a vehicle for teaching children how to make inferences. They contend that doing so is one way of explicitly showing students how to interact with a spoken message.

Since the structured listening guide will ask your students to listen to you without some of the previous structural supports you used during whole-class lessons (i.e., name cards, class lists, and interactive guides), you'll want to reflect on their initial ability to infer from spoken texts. After using an initial structured listening guide, you can reflect on the students' abilities to process texts as they are listening. You can compare these results with recent performances with similar whole-class texts you presented with teacher supports. This will let you answer two questions: First, were students able to become more independent with their listening after using and reducing the use of teacher supports? Second, what were students' baseline levels to independently use listening to think deeply about text? With a structured listening guide focused on inferring, you can also use their responses to the structured listening guide to specifically examine their ability to contribute literal, interpretative, and applied responses. Repeating the activity with texts containing similar demands and reflecting on subsequent performances will allow you to see changes in their processing.

What Can You Use to Make Progress in Meeting This Goal?

You can follow a set of guidelines that provide teaching suggestions to plan a structured listening guide to use with your students to help them learn how to make inferences while listening to a text (Opitz and Zbaracki 2004; Alvermann 1984). (See Figure 1–7.)

First, choose a text from one of the content areas you will be addressing. Then review the text to construct a guide for your use. Keep it simple to start. Identify declarative statements that represent different levels of comprehension: literal, interpretive, and applied. Try to find three examples of each level. Also, intentionally select at least three points where you will stop when you are reading the text. Each stop should represent a different level of comprehension. The *literal level* demands that students focus on what is actually stated in the text. At the *interpretive level*, students are more actively involved in inferring because they have to reason beyond what is directly stated in the text. At the *applied level*, students talk about how the text or an event from the text relates to their lives.

To begin the lesson, set the purpose for the whole listening experience by stating the three literal statements related to the text. Then read the entire text. Revisit the three literal statements that you made prior to reading the book and provide time for your students to respond. Then provide students with statements at the interpretive level and time for discussion. Finally provide students with statements at the applied level and time for discussion. Conclude the listening session by discussing why listening and making inferences is important.

How Else Can You Use This Technique to Accelerate Instruction?

There are at least three other ways that a structured listening guide can be used to accelerate instruction for your students. First, remember that the guide is flexible. You can begin with the applied level, then move to the literal level, and finally end with the interpretive level. Also, you can adapt the guide depending on your students' ages and abilities. You can work toward eliminating specific statements to guide the listening and use generic questions to prompt children to talk about the text. Using the guide in this manner accelerates instruction because you only spend time on what your students actually need. The remaining time can be devoted to other needed content.

Second, you can use a variation of this guide that provides some statements that are either true or partially true. Read the statements aloud prior to reading the story. Then tell your students that they are to listen to the story to determine which of the statements are true and which are partially true. After reading the story, revisit each statement and provide time for the students to share their ideas. You can also encourage students to use the text to verify clues that led them to respond as they did.

Finally, in using some books, such as *Train* (Cooper 2013), you can invite your students to infer—to fill in the gaps in the story. For example, in the book the train leaves after passengers purchase their tickets. But where are the tickets purchased and how? Your students can fill in the gaps by talking about their own experiences with seeing people buy tickets either online or at a ticket counter.

Since your students will be asked to process other types of texts beyond read-aloud situations, you can also develop structured listening guides for programs students are watching or for other oral presentations, like those given by guest speakers.

elle selects *Bullies Never Win* (Cuyler 2009), a text to help students learn to make inferences while simultaneously learning more about bullying. Using the procedures listed earlier, she constructs a listening guide (see Figure 1–8). Before reading the book to the children, she comments, "The book I am going to read to you today is *Bullies Never Win*, by Margery Cuyler. These are some ideas the author tells you about bullying:

1. Jessica worries night and day.
2. Jessica has one main worry.
3. Jessica stands up for herself to get rid of her biggest worry.

"Please listen to the story. If I come to a part that tells why Jessica worries, what her main worry is, or how Jessica stands up for herself to get rid of her worry, please raise your hand. I will then stop and give you time to turn, talk, and listen to your neighbor and then ask for volunteers to share."

Elle then reads the story and calls on volunteers using name cards to make sure that she gives equal opportunities for all to share.

After reading, she comments, "You did an excellent job of listening to what the author said about Jessica's worry and how she got rid of it. Now I want you to pretend that you are detectives and tell how much courage it took for Jessica to solve her worry. Just like detectives use clues to solve their problems, I want you to tell me what clues you used from the story to tell how Jessica used courage to solve her worry. Turn, talk, and listen to your partner."

After providing time for students to share their ideas and clues, Elle states, "You have shown that you can do two things when you listen to a story. You showed that you could listen to exactly what the author stated. You also showed that you can put the pieces together to understand what the author wanted you to understand even though she didn't exactly tell you. You showed how you used clues to understand how Jessica was courageous. Now I want you to show how you can use what you already know to help you understand how Jessica was feeling. Listen as I read this sentence: 'Toothpicks may be thin, but bullies never win.' Think about a time when you had to use courage to resolve a problem and how you felt about yourself."

Elle has students think and share with their partners; they discuss their answers as a group; and she concludes by telling her students that sometimes listeners have to think very carefully about what the author is saying and not directly saying to best understand a text.

Figure 1–7 Structured Listening Guide Planning Sheet

Structured Listening Guide Planning Sheet

Text:	Potential Literal Evidence	Potential Interpretive Prompt(s)	Potential Applied Prompt(s)
Literal Statement 1			
Literal Statement 2			
Literal Statement 3			

Figure 1–8 Sample Structured Listening Guide Planning Sheet			
Text: *Bullies Never Win*, by Margery Cuyler	**Potential Literal Evidence** These are some ideas the author tells you about bullying.	**Potential Interpretive Prompt(s)** I want you to pretend that you are detectives and tell how much courage it took for Jessica to solve her worry. Just like detectives use clues to solve their problems, I want you to tell me what clues you used from the story to tell how Jessica used courage to solve her worry.	**Potential Applied Prompt(s)** Now I want you to show how you can use what you already know to help you understand how Jessica was feeling. Listen as I read this sentence: "Toothpicks may be thin, but bullies never win." Think about a time when you had to use courage to resolve a problem and how you felt about yourself.
Literal Statement 1 Jessica worries night and day.	Please listen to the story. If I come to a part that tells why Jessica worries, raise your hand.		
Literal Statement 2 Jessica has one main worry.	Please listen to the story. If I come to a part that tells what her main worry is, raise your hand.		
Literal Statement 3 Jessica stands up for herself to get rid of her biggest worry.	Please listen to the story. If I come to a part that tells how Jessica stands up for herself to get rid of her worry, please raise your hand.		

Directed Listening-Thinking Activities (DLTAs)

What Is the Goal?

The goal is to engage all students in a directed listening-thinking activity (Rubin 2000) to show them how important it is to make and change predictions when acquiring ongoing information when listening (and reading!).

Why Is the Goal Important?

Making predictions is one important comprehension strategy. The ability to do so shows that readers are engaging with the text and making meaning along the way. Competent readers are continually making predictions and confirming or changing them as they continue to read a given text. It requires students to use past experiences in combination with the new information in a selection or talk to make logical guesses (i.e., predictions) about the content of the story or the talk. After making predictions, students then listen to confirm or change their predictions based on what they hear. Students are more apt to be able to use this important skill during reading if they learn how to use it when listening. Listening requires a little less effort in that students have no need to decode words as they do when reading. Instead, their entire energy is focused on ascertaining information through listening.

How Can You Evaluate Your Current Efforts in Meeting This Goal?

A directed listening-thinking activity is one way to help students learn to make predictions. The discussion occurs before, during, and after the story to help students better understand how to make and monitor predictions throughout. One of your major goals is to help the students understand that making predictions is ongoing rather than a onetime event. Another goal is to help your students see that making predictions is one way to stay involved in the story, making understanding more likely. The DLTA is also adaptable for use when your students are watching a visual "text" or listening to an oral presentation. One way to evaluate whether your students are able to make predictions is to pose questions throughout the reading and note what students say. If their comments are close to the author's intended meaning, you can assume that students are making accurate predictions.

What Can You Use to Make Progress in Meeting This Goal?

Following are several specific teaching suggestions you can use to enable success for your students and yourself:

1. Prepare for a presentation, which can take many forms, such as listening to a story, a talk, an audiotape, or a CD, or watching a video or a DVD. To best prepare, relate the current presentation with listeners' past experiences, provide an overview, present any unique vocabulary, and pose questions at different difficulty levels.
2. Share with students that the purpose for listening is to help them learn more about making and using predictions.
3. Read the text or make the presentation as students listen for answers to some of the questions posed earlier.
4. Stop at various points and ask students whether or not they have answers to any of the posed questions. At each stopping point, ask some additional questions to guide students' listening.
5. Read to the next stopping point and, once again, discuss any answers to posed questions and make new predictions.
6. After the text or presentation is finished, provide time for children to answer any unanswered questions. You can then ask additional challenging questions and ask students to state the central idea of the talk and give a short summary of it.
7. As an optional step, invite students to create some questions that could be used in subsequent readings of the text.
8. Remind students that making predictions is important because it can help them to stay focused on the message the speaker is trying to communicate. Making predictions and listening to confirm or modify them is also a way to stay actively involved with the story or the talk.

How Else Can You Use This Technique to Accelerate Instruction?

Three additional ways you can use listening to enhance students' abilities to make predictions are as follows:

1. To help students become comfortable with making predictions in all subject areas, provide time for them to preread questions and make some predictions about possible answers. After listening, students can return to the questions and talk about which, if any, have been answered.
2. You can also use the sneak preview technique (DeHaven 1989), which provides a slight variation of the DLTA. After reading or telling

part of a story or event, stop and have the students think about what they heard and make illustrations showing their predictions of the next event. Invite your students to share their pictures and tell why they think the predicted events might happen. Continue the reading and have students confirm their predictions.

3. Another instructional strategy you can use is ELVES (excite, listen, visualize, extend, savor; Levesque 1989). Begin with a discussion that connects the listeners' personal experiences that are appropriate to the text. Then ask listeners to make predictions about the text using cues from the previous discussion and by looking at the book cover and title (i.e., get listeners *excited* for the activity). Next, have students *listen* to the text and simultaneously think about their predictions. Also invite children to *visualize* while listening to the text. These visualizations will be used for discussion. Fourth, *extend* the text by asking questions that encourage deeper thinking about it. Finally, ask listeners to *savor* and reflect on the text and connect it with their lives.

All of these options provide ways to accelerate instruction because they call on students to apply their listening comprehension skills. As mentioned before, application is a higher-order thinking skill that calls on learners to internalize or think more deeply about their learning. Consequently, less time is needed for repetition to learn specific skills, which you can utilize to teach other content.

Elle uses *Strong Man: The Story of Charles Atlas* (McCarthy 2007) when constructing a DLTA to help her students learn how to make predictions and how to set goals simultaneously. After setting the purpose for listening, she asks students to share their experiences with achieving something they really wanted to accomplish and how they actually accomplished that goal. After providing time for students to think, pair, and share, she uses name cards to call on students to share their thoughts. She then shows students the book and asks them to make some predictions using their previous discussion and by looking at the cover of the book. Elle then begins reading the story and stops after the first few pages, asking, "What have we already learned about Charles? What do you think he will do next? How do you know?" She turns the page and uses the picture to confirm students' predictions. She continues reading, stopping along the way and asking, "What do you think will happen now?" (See Figure 1–9 for stopping points and questions Elle poses.)

To bring the DLTA to a close, Elle asks students to summarize what happened and how Charles Atlas set and achieved his goal. She uses the class list to monitor and note how individual students participate when summarizing with their sharing partners.

Figure 1–9 Stopping Points for *Strong Man* DLTA

Page Number(s)	Prompt
Page 6	Who helped Angelo set a goal of becoming stronger? Why was being stronger important to him?
Pages 9 and 10	After looking at the illustrations and the text above them, what do you think they tell you about setting goals? What information is left out that you might need to know in order to achieve your goals?
Page 11	Was it a goal of Angelo's to be named Charles Atlas, or did others impose it onto him?
Pages 21 and 22	What are three ways that Charles Atlas helped others to achieve their fitness goals?
Pages 28 and 29	What are some exercises you might set a goal to achieve?

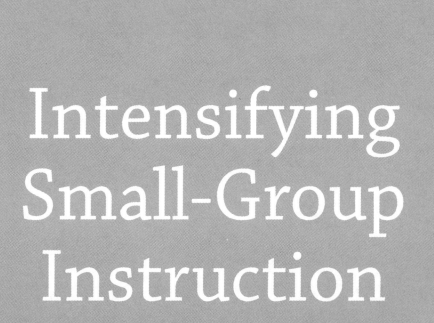

Intensifying
Small-Group
Instruction

Students are social beings,

and this is apparent both in and out of the classroom. Just as they crave social interaction on the playground, when in the classroom, discussion and collaboration are natural parts of a student's learning and development, and students will readily embrace collaboration with peers as a reason to read.

ANGELA McRAE AND JOHN T. GUTHRIE,
"PROMOTING REASONS FOR READING:
TEACHER PRACTICES THAT IMPACT MOTIVATION"

e d knows that using small groups offers him better opportunities to support his students as learners than exclusively using whole-group instruction. He believes in the value of small groups to actively involve more learners by giving them more chances to discuss and collaborate with each other. He can help students take more responsibility for what they learn by using instructional models based on small groups. He can more effectively provide feedback tailored to group members.

With twenty-four diverse learners in his class, he also knows that the use of small groups can be a bit daunting, but he doesn't let that stop him from giving it a try. He looks at the reading on habitats in the text for the day. The text is broken up with headings, which helps him see that he can have different groups read different parts. In other words, the text can be jigsawed. He has learned that instead of pulling everyone through the whole text, he can divide it into parts. He can strategically assign different parts of the text to different groups of students. He also has multiple copies of related trade books on different types of habitats. Instead of having everyone read about every major type of habitat, he can give one set to each group to allow the groups to explore and extend the information in the class text more deeply as they each become experts on one of the major types of habitats.

Before Ed focuses on helping one group, he successfully prepares texts and tasks for all the remaining small groups, which will read and respond more independently. It feels a bit like managing a difficult juggling act. Once prepared, he is finally ready to engage all groups and decides to sit with the group he knows will need his support the most. While sitting with the group, however, he finds himself unable to focus as he tries to monitor the other groups from a distance. As they operate away from him, he sees one group struggling to get started, another off to a good start but not including all members in the group task, and the other group quickly racing to complete the task. He predicts they will say they are finished before he has time to fully attend to the group he is sitting with. He gets the group he is working with on track and begins dropping in on the other groups to monitor their efforts. A quick assessment leaves him a little disappointed. In the end, as the students report out for their groups, Ed realizes the instruction fell short of capturing the thinking and excitement he was expecting as outcomes.

Why Is It Important to Strengthen Small-Group Instruction?

No matter how good whole-group instruction is, using small groups enables us to put learners who are more alike than different together to focus instruction on similar needs or capitalize on similar interests. As we can see with Ed, differentiating instruction becomes more doable than daunting if teachers can use instructional models that allow for varying of groups, texts, and levels of support. Ed is combining two models we have explored in the past. He first uses a jigsawed whole-class text, which allows him to more effectively match chunks of the text that may vary in terms of their literacy demands, conceptual loads, and stamina needs to his strategically planned groups. In Appendix B we provide a planning guide that you can use to plan a jigsawed lesson. Then Ed moves toward the use of a connected text set with multiple copies, so he can also match groups of texts to groups of kids. We have described this model as connected literature circles (Opitz and Ford 2008). In Appendix C, we provide a planning guide that can assist teachers like Ed to intentionally plan the members, texts, and levels of support for each group.

Remember that it's not the use of small groups to instruct that will guarantee accelerated growth of all learners. It's how you use the small groups. The power of the small group comes from the ability of the teacher and students to support one another as they think and talk deeply about the texts. Powerful learning comes as a result of students collaborating and cooperating to complete the small-group tasks.

But there are challenges. When the teacher is with a given group, mediation of the text requires the attention of both the teacher and the students.

Distraction of either or both will lessen the impact of the small group. Groups that spend most of their time managing themselves instead of reading, thinking, and talking about the texts will be less likely to gain much from the small-group work. Small groups dominated by a few group members while others sit back will be limited in producing powerful outcomes for all. Finally, those that see quickness and quality as equally valuable and spend most of their group time wondering what to do next will also fall a bit short of achieving the most powerful outcomes.

Five Classroom Catalysts for Intensifying Small-Group Instruction

To accelerate the growth of all learners while using small groups, we need to consider how to tighten up instruction both while a small group is working with the teacher and, maybe even more importantly, while it is working away from the teacher. In this section we present five classroom catalysts for accelerating the growth of all learners in addressing key issues within small-group instruction:

1. Discussion matrices
2. Small-group taping and analysis
3. Warm-up cards
4. Picture walk alternatives
5. Word count boosters

We frame our discussion of each catalyst around five questions:

1. What is the goal?
2. Why is the goal important?
3. How can you evaluate your current efforts in meeting this goal?
4. What can you use to make progress in meeting this goal?
5. How else can you use this technique to accelerate instruction?

For each catalyst, we also provide classroom examples and appropriate support materials for you to use with your students.

As with the ideas we presented for whole-group instruction in Section 1, each of the ideas here can stand alone. However, rather than seeing these five ideas as separate activities, we encourage you to see them as interrelated—a collective effort to tighten up small-group instruction to accelerate the growth of all learners. Combining one or more of the ideas for any given lesson will provide you with acceleration tools to capture, analyze, and improve how students think about and discuss the texts they are learning from. The discussion matrix provides a tool by which you can analyze the thinking and strategy use behind the language used in text discussions. Instructional acceleration continues when you transfer the responsibility to the students to operate effectively by themselves. Techniques like small-group taping and analysis enable students to think more independently and deeply about their thinking, language, and strategy use. As with whole-group instruction, instructional acceleration still depends on maximizing every minute of instruction in the small group. Engagement remains important, and instructional supports like warm-up cards add instructional time to small-group transitions. Instructional acceleration also requires you to think about balance in the instruction as you try to spend as much time as possible coaching students during reading. Picture walk alternatives can help you focus on teaching learners in addition to texts. Finally, instructional acceleration still relies on quality opportunities to practice. You can be more intentional about addressing issues around practice with guidelines for word count boosters.

Discussion Matrices

What Is the Goal?

To accelerate the growth of all learners in small-group settings, maintaining high-quality independent student discussions is critical, especially when those conversations take place away from the teacher. You can begin by assessing where your students' baseline levels of language, thinking, strategy use, and social interaction are when they work together in student-driven small groups. Then you can structure small-group instruction to maximize the performance of all students to provide evidence of expanded language, deeper thinking, enhanced strategy use, and more appropriate student interactions. In a gradual release model, the first goal is to model language, thought, strategy use, and interaction techniques so that when you are working with small groups, students are able to demonstrate those competencies with you first and ultimately away from you.

Why Is the Goal Important?

One size does not fit all. Teachers need to use a variety of grouping practices. They have to get comfortable using small groups flexibly to more effectively meet the needs and interests of their students. Small groups provide more opportunities to vary the texts, the members, and the level of teacher support with the student groups. Since you can't be with all groups at the same time, you need to raise your comfort level that when groups are meeting away from you, they are operating with a level of confidence and especially competence, maximizing the instructional time they spend working together.

Small groups provide the best opportunities for more students to read, think, talk, and write about texts and topics. It is their levels of talk and writing (and the use of other expressive arts) that reveal their levels of thinking and ability to *use* strategies. You need to monitor small-group responses to inform your thinking about what you can do next to help your students read more closely and think more deeply about what they are learning.

How Can You Evaluate Your Current Efforts in Meeting This Goal?

Small-group discussions are loaded with data, but teachers often do very little to capture these data. You need to systematically try to capture the flow of your students' discussion of the text when you are conferring with them. You need to come into the group with a clear focus on what you need to listen for in their conversations to analyze what kind of thinking is reflected in their language and what kind of strategies are at the heart of their thinking. To do so, prepare a Discussion Matrix (see Figure 2–1) with key strategies listed down the side and the names of the students in the group across the top. Tell your kids that today you are going to just be a listener and an observer for the group. As the students begin to talk about the text, use a simple coding system to track which students are contributing to the discussion and flow and what kind(s) of strategies are embedded in their language and thought. This will allow you to capture a baseline on the social dynamics, language, thinking, and strategy use in that group with that type of text. Remember that these data will grow stronger the more times you use techniques like these.

What Can You Use to Make Progress in Meeting This Goal?

Once you know what your students' discussions reveal about their language, thinking, and strategy use, you will have a better sense of how to structure your focus lessons before students move into their small groups and how to target instruction with groups when you meet with them. For instance, think about a strategy like making connections. As you go into the group, listen carefully for what kinds of connections your students make as they talk about texts. Do they mainly make connections to themselves? Do they ever make connections between and among other texts? Do they ever bring in connections from the outside world? If you gather information only related to making connections during their work, in the end you may spot a pattern. If you see that your students frequently make text-to-self connections but rarely use text-to-text or text-to-world connections, you can shift your modeling and probing to provide an additional direction for their thinking and talk. You can even give students some direction and language prompts to help scaffold the talk in new directions.

How Else Can You Use This Technique to Accelerate Instruction?

You can design the grid to focus on specific strategy use within specific genres. For example, if students are discussing narrative texts, you can design the grid to focus exclusively on which literary elements of narrative stories the students discuss, like characters, setting, theme, plot, conflict, and resolution.

The more you try to move students to deeper thought and understanding, the more you'll start seeing the complexity of the strategies being used.

Therefore, you may need to develop a more sophisticated coding system to analyze the type of knowledge reflected in the students' language and strategy use. For example:

Level 0: No awareness of the strategy.

Level 1: Declarative knowledge (what)—talked about but not used. They know what the strategy is but give no evidence of how or when to use it.

Level 2: Procedural knowledge (how)—inconsistent use. They know what the strategy is and how to use it but give evidence of only inconsistent use.

Level 3: Conditional knowledge (why)—consistent, appropriate use. They know what the strategy is, how to use it, and why to use it and give evidence of consistent successful use.

To focus in on a specific strategy, such as using visualization to make meaning, listen carefully to the language being used to reflect the thinking of the students and code comments to show the level of understanding of the strategy:

Level 0: Language and thought do not reveal use of visualization even for literal understanding of text.

Level 1: Language and thought reveal use of visualization to communicate literal understanding of text.

Level 2: Language and thought reveal use of visualization to communicate main concepts and demonstrate inferences about the text.

Level 3: Language and thought go beyond just visual images to use all senses to understand the text.

Once you have gathered information about your students, you can accelerate instruction by using it to design meaningful instruction focusing your time and energy on what students need to know rather than using your already limited classroom time on what students already know. For example, if your data show that students have some idea about using visualizing (level 1), rather than taking time for an introductory lesson, you can skip ahead and design lessons that provide additional information (levels 2 and 3) and have students call forth what they already know as a starting place.

ed decides to focus his observation when he interacts with his small groups. He has grown in his confidence that the data he has been collecting and analyzing from use of the Discussion Matrices (Figure 2–1) and Student Analysis Grids (Figure 2–2) have started to show patterns in the language, thinking, strategy use, and interaction techniques of his students. He has been able to see these patterns when he has used the grids to analyze what the groups have reported out and in their written responses to texts. It's clear that with nonfiction, his students can restate what the texts have to say but fall short of making important inferences leading to critical questioning, even though he has selected articles that allude to how certain man-made activities are threatening natural habitats.

Now Ed wants students to read with greater depth. He wants to see if his students can add more thoughtful layers to their discussions. Before moving his students into their small groups for the day, Ed selects a news article about artificial encroachment on the Great Barrier Reef. He reads it aloud, using a think-aloud as he reads between the lines and surfaces a bottom-line critical question for him. He focuses the students on digging deeper into their articles in a similar way before moving them into their small groups. He observes the talk as he moves between each group.

With quick prompts, he brings groups back to the discussion he has modeled. Once confident that all groups are on task, he sits between two groups that are having a hard time getting started. He turns his attention to one group to provide a more direct reminder of what he has modeled in the focus lesson. Doing so pays off as the group is then able to get focused on the task at hand. Then he turns his attention to the other group to provide more direct support in helping the students read closely, dig deeper, and find critical questions they can share when the groups report out.

As the groups report out, he listens closely to the language students use and thinks about the strategies that students appear to be using. He uses his discussion matrix to complete the student analysis grid to capture the data. Doing so enables him to see a pattern that shows students' ability to use greater depth in exploring and reacting to the content of the text. By knowing how to focus his front-end instruction and tasks for the groups, he has been able to accelerate instruction by monitoring each group and intervening with appropriate prompts and supports.

Figure 2–1 Discussion Matrix

Discussion Matrix

Directions: As you meet with a small group of students discussing a text or multiple texts, use the discussion matrix to capture the type of strategy use reflected in the language and thinking of the students. Place the names of the students across the top of the grid. Use a plus sign (+) to indicate what strategy is reflected in a comment made by a student. Use a minus sign (–) to indicate confusion about strategy use as reflected in a student's comment. After the discussion is completed, use the Student Analysis Grid (Figure 2–2) to analyze the information captured on the discussion matrix (the nature of the interaction).

Strategy	Student 1 _____	Student 2 _____	Student 3 _____	Student 4 _____	Student 5 _____	Student 6 _____	Other Observations About Strategy
Ask and Answer Questions							
Determine Important Information							
Make Connections							
Monitor Comprehension							
Predict							
Summarize							
Visualize							
Other Observations About Students							

Figure 2–2 Student Analysis Grid

Student Analysis Grid

Directions: Use the completed discussion matrix to complete this student analysis grid. Start by looking at which members contributed and how often. Then analyze the quality of the interactions. Think about what strategies were apparent in the oral comments of the students. Reflect on these three questions to inform your thinking about what to plan before returning to the small-group work:

- How might the dynamic of the discussion need to be improved?
- How might the content of the discussion need to be improved?
- What adjustments should be made for instruction prior to the next round of small-group discussion?

Repeat the process so the data collected grow in strength and reveal more stability in patterns of students' talk, thought, and strategy use.

Student	Number of Comments Made	Quality of Comments

Figure 2–2 *Continued*

Student Analysis Grid

Student	Number of Comments Made	Quality of Comments

Small-Group Taping and Analysis

What Is the Goal?

You can take pride in any improvement of language, thinking, strategy use, and interactive techniques your students show in small groups, but if those outcomes are primarily driven by teacher direction, management, and support, your goal needs to evolve. It's time to shift from teacher-directed small-group work to student-driven small-group work. You want to see an internalized way of talking and responding to texts in your students that operates whether you are present or not. It's time to move your students from guided practice to independent use (Pearson and Gallagher 1983).

Why Is the Goal Important?

You will not always be present to focus, prompt, and support the language, thinking, strategy use, and interactive techniques of your students. Therefore, to accelerate student learning, you need to always teach for transfer (Dorn and Soffos 2011). When you remove yourself from the context, you want students to be able to carry on. In other words, when the context for learning changes, students should be able to draw from what they have previously learned and transfer it to the new context. If students see their learning as situated in the context in which the instruction takes place or as something they do only when they are with the teacher, transfer breaks down. This lack of transfer thwarts accelerated learning because what was learned ends up having very limited use and application.

College and career readiness standards (NGA Center for Best Practices and CCSSO 2010) suggest that students should be able to "engage effectively in a range of collaborative discussions (one-on-one, in groups, and teacher-led) with diverse partners on [grade-level] topics and texts, building on others' ideas and expressing their own clearly" (see, for example, CCSS.ELA-Literacy .SL.3.1). These standards recommend that students should at least be able to do the following:

CCSS.ELA-Literacy.SL.3.1a: Come to discussions prepared, having read or studied required material; explicitly draw on that preparation and other information known about the topic to explore ideas under discussion.

CCSS.ELA-Literacy.SL.3.1b: Follow agreed-upon rules for discussions and carry out assigned roles.

CCSS.ELA-Literacy.SL.3.1c: Pose and respond to specific questions to clarify or follow up on information, and make comments that contribute to the discussion and link to the remarks of others.

CCSS.ELA-Literacy.SL.3.1d: Review the key ideas expressed and explain their own ideas and understanding in light of the discussion.

Similar standards are recommended for grades K–12. If your discussions are always teacher led, then your students will not grow in their expertise to effectively interact in one-on-one and small-group discussions independently. If you lead a discussion, the class will likely fall back into that common I-R-E classroom pattern—you'll initiate, one or two students will respond, and you will be so happy to get any response that you will quickly praise the answers and move on. The way to break out of that tiresome language pattern is to get yourself out of the way. Others have found that interaction patterns change when grouping patterns change and students are allowed to talk to one another (Cohen 1994; Youngs 2012).

How Can You Evaluate Your Current Efforts in Meeting This Goal?

If you are going to evaluate your current efforts in moving your students toward independence in the ways they talk, think, use strategies, and interact, you'll need to remove yourself from the context. You cannot disappear completely, but try to remove yourself as much as possible. Ask each group to use a simple recording device to record its discussion. Once the group discussions are recorded, collect the devices to analyze the discussions that took place away from you. (Watching technology evolve is interesting. Lightspeed, a company that develops miking systems for classroom teachers, now has a tool called Flexcat that allows a teacher to sit at a console and place remote mikes at students' tables. The teacher can then "drop in" on a group conversation by remotely turning on the table's mike without being present at the table.) Continue to use Discussion Matrices and Student Analysis Grids (Figures 2–1 and 2–2) that you used to analyze teacher-led discussions. The tools that you used when you were present to listen to the groups can now be used to obtain baseline data on their independent levels of language, thought, strategy use, and interactive techniques. Once baseline levels are established, you can use this procedure to measure whether these independent behaviors are improving.

Eventually, students should be able to monitor their discussions independently. After analyzing the recorded student discussions, you'll have a baseline on their abilities to discuss independently. You'll get a good sense of what the interaction pattern is like when you are not present and managing the group. Look closely at the language of the discussion, and the thinking and strategy use it reflects. The best way to help students make progress in these areas is to get them involved in the process.

You can begin this process by involving the students in generating a set of guidelines that will help them have a clear set of expectations for small-group work, whether it is being done with or away from you. (See Figure 2–3 for an example set of guidelines.) Be mindful of assuming they know what effective small-group interaction looks like, sounds like, or feels like.

While a clear list of expectations can be helpful, that in and of itself will not be enough. These rules will need to be internalized in the thinking and talk of the group's members. So why not have students listen to one of their recorded discussions? After having a chance to listen in, you can meet with the group. Replay the recording and ask your students to listen to their discussion. Initially, they may just listen to focus on their own contribution and learning (see Figure 2–4). The self-evaluation techniques may raise the attention of some group members and bring some accountability to the teamwork. Individual self-evaluation can then shift to group evaluations. The group members can begin at a global level, thinking about how they would rate dimensions like the collective quality of speaking, listening, participation, and respect. You can use rubrics to guide the group evaluation (see Figure 2–5 for an example). Eventually, you can teach your students to track the interaction pattern of the group and talk about how the social interaction might be improved. You can make a few adjustments to the Student Analysis Grid to create a Small-Group Taping and Analysis Grid for groups to use (see Figure 2–6 for an example). Use teachable moments to point out when students questioned and extended the thinking of others. Identify specific language prompts—perhaps even write them down and display them for the class—as models to enhance future discussions (see Figure 2–7 for an example list).

Students can also fine-tune their ability to listen to their language about the text. With guidance, they can learn how to self-evaluate what their comments reflect about their thinking and strategy use and how they might push themselves to think more deeply about the text and to consider new ways of responding to the text. This will help them move their thought and talk in new directions.

You'll want to engage students in other ways to respond to their texts. Discussion groups and oral language may not be the only way to reveal close readings and deep thought. Students can use similar self-evaluation processes to look at their written responses. Students should learn to ask, "What did my written comments reveal about my thinking, and what strategies did I use?" as you open up options for your students to use multimodal responses. These response projects may involve more than just written and oral responses but also production of visual images captured in art, film, photography, graphic design, or dance. Those response projects can also be analyzed with similar critical questions. While self-evaluation is not a new technique, it is often used to more globally assess the outcome. In this case, you can try instead (or additionally) to push their assessments to look more closely at the thinking beyond product creation (be it oral, written, or visual).

Perhaps the main way that this technique accelerates instruction and learning is that it provides students with a heightened sense of ownership over their learning, which connects to the motivation generalizations stated on page xvi in the introduction of this book.

Yesterday, Ed conducted a brief focus lesson involving all members in the group discussion. He gave his students some language models they could use to agree with, build on, or politely question a comment of another member of the group. He asked a small group of students to role-play an imbalanced interaction and then use the language prompts to show an example of a more balanced interaction. He quickly discussed with the students what made the second discussion more effective. He challenged the students in each group to think about what they saw when they started their discussion for the day. He placed recording devices with each group so he could review their discussions later on.

Afterward, Ed used the recording devices to listen to the discussions. He decided that less might be more, so he listened carefully to each, trying to capture the essence of the flow of conversation that the role-playing group modeled before he had students break up into their small groups. While concerned with the depth of thinking and level of language in the discussions, he decided to first focus on getting all learners engaged in the small-group discussion. Once he has raised the levels of participation of all students, especially when the groups are working away from him, he will start to focus more on the quality of the conversations.

Now, as groups disperse, Ed chooses to sit with one of his groups. He asks each student to listen carefully as he replays their discussion from the previous day. Each student makes a list of the group members' names. They tally each time a student makes a comment and use a plus sign if the comment really encouraged interaction (affirmed, built on, or questioned another student), a minus sign if the comment seemed inappropriate, or a star for a really insightful comment.

After listening to the discussion and making their appropriate markings next to each group member's name, the students count the marks they have recorded and reflect on how different students contributed to the discussion. Ed then passes out a rubric and engages students in a group evaluation of their performance in terms of listening, speaking, participation, and respect. Before leaving the group, he has group members reflect on three key questions that could improve their efforts for the next round of discussions: How does the dynamic of our discussion need to be improved? How does the content of our discussion need to be improved? How should we focus our reading and discussion next time?

Figure 2–3 Discussion Etiquette

1. Use appropriate body posture and eye contact to focus on the discussion.
2. Actively participate (e.g., respond to ideas, share when appropriate).
3. Ask questions for clarification as needed.
4. Expand on others' ideas and thoughts.
5. Disagree constructively.
6. Listen actively.
7. Take turns letting others speak.
8. Support opinions with evidence.
9. Encourage others.

Figure 2–4 Small-Group Discussion Evaluation

Small-Group Discussion Evaluation

Your Name: _____ Date: _____ Group: _____

On a scale of 1–5, with 1 being poor and 5 being excellent, please rate your group or yourself.

Characteristic	Rating
1. All group members appeared to have read the assigned material.	
2. All group members contributed to the conversation.	
3. All group members used these group strategies: • • • • •	
4. I participated about the right amount, that is, not too much or too little.	
5. Here's one contribution I made:	
6. Something I learned more about was . . .	

Figure 2–5 Sample Group Evaluation Rubric

Sample Group Evaluation Rubric

Listening	We were paying attention to each other by listening to what others were saying and responding to questions.	We were paying attention most of the time but may have been distracted a few times.	We were distracted more often than we were paying attention.
Speaking	We had thoughtful insights about the text and shared them with each other. We expressed our ideas about the text in order to get feedback.	We had insights but did not explore or explain them fully to the group.	We did not share our insights with the group.
Participation	We did the assigned reading and preparation. We were engaged in the discussion.	We did most of the work and were engaged most of the time in the discussion.	We were not prepared and were not engaged in the discussion.
Respect	We listened to our classmates' ideas with open minds, complimented each other on a job well done, and did *not* put each other down. We also took turns talking so everyone had a chance to participate.	We listened to our classmates most of the time and avoided put-downs. We took turns most of the time.	We did not listen to our classmates, did not compliment each other, and did use put-downs. We did not take turns.

Figure 2–6 Small-Group Taping and Analysis Grid

Small-Group Taping and Analysis Grid

Directions

1. Preview the recording using the small-group Discussion Matrix and the Student Analysis Grid (see Figures 2–1 and 2–2).
2. Jot down two to three key aspects of the discussion you want to point out to the students when you return to work with the group, reflecting on these questions: How does the dynamic of the discussion need to be improved? and How does the content of the discussion need to be improved? Listen for both global adjustments that could be made as well as specific language patterns that you want to highlight.
3. Return to the small group. Invite the students to listen carefully to the previously conducted discussion. Provide them with a rubric such as the one shown in Figure 2–5 to guide their self-evaluation of the discussion on global dimensions.
4. After students have listened to the discussion, have them mark their rubrics. Guide them in a discussion about how they felt about the quality of speaking, listening, participation, and respect and what steps they could take to improve their interactions.
5. Eventually introduce the students to this small-group taping and analysis form. Students can begin by tracking their own talk and the thinking it reflects. As they track themselves, they can identify the steps they would take to improve their contributions in future discussions. Then they can be guided to track the discussion of the entire group and see how their contributions worked with their classmates'.

• How does the dynamic of our discussion need to be improved?

• How does the content of our discussion need to be improved?

• How should we focus our reading and discussion next time?

continues

Figure 2–6 *Continued*

Small-Group Taping and Analysis Grid

Student	Number of Comments Made	Nature of Comments

Figure 2–7 Language Prompts to Use When Responding to Texts in Groups

- I liked/disliked _____ because . . .

- I wonder why . . .

- I have a connection to . . .

- I think the author's message is . . .

- To add on to _____'s thought, . . .

- That's a good thought, but I still think . . .

- Can you give me more evidence?

- Can you explain that more?

- Why do you think that?

Warm-Up Cards

What Is the Goal?

As the effectiveness of your universal instruction grows in the large-group setting, and the independent small-group work of your students grows more powerful, you can turn your attention to using small groups for classroom interventions. Intervention groups allow a forum for providing targeted instruction needed by some in a class. As when using small groups for other purposes, these groups should reflect high levels of engagement and efficient use of instructional time.

Why Is the Goal Important?

Instructional time is just as critical in small groups as it is in the large group. In fact, as you juggle meeting with your intervention groups, instructional time may be even more critical. Researchers have revealed that teachers report spending twenty-two minutes on average when they meet with their small reading groups (Ford and Opitz 2008). Even a small amount of wasted transitional time as kids move to and from the small-group work station each day can add up to a significant amount—and that is time you need for instruction.

Just like the challenge of working with them in the large group, you also need to keep all kids engaged while they are working with you in a small group. Even when working with a small group of children who are of similar achievement levels, you will need to give individual students individual attention. Research shows that effective coaching while students are reading may be the most important element of instruction. Coaching seems to make a difference between those teachers who are most effective and those who are moderately or least effective (Taylor et al. 1999). Keep in mind—especially in your intervention groups—that the goal is to teach the *learners* how to use texts to their best advantage.

How Can You Evaluate Your Current Efforts in Meeting This Goal?

To gain a sense of how you are doing with targeting instruction in your classroom-based small-group interventions, try taping a few of your sessions.

Start the tape as soon as you indicate to group members that you need to meet with them at the small-group table. The first information you can collect is how much time is consumed by the transition. You can see this from the running timer on the recording device. Then monitor your interactions with students as you track the instructional interaction you have with each individual. Analyze the degree of engagement for each individual by attending to the verbal and nonverbal indicators. Finally, look at your ability to tailor instruction to individuals by listening a second time to your responses as you try to coach during the small-group work. The Intervention Analysis Grid (Figure 2–8) might help you initially capture this data and allow you to revisit your performance to self-assess for improvement.

What Can You Use to Make Progress in Meeting This Goal?

Prepare a set of task cards to have ready for your intervention groups. As students come to the small-group work area, hand each student one of those cards, intentionally selected to engage the student immediately in a warm-up activity. Provide each student with a targeted warm-up activity until the final student arrives at the table. These tasks should be based on identified coaching targets from the previous session (see Figure 2–9). As the students are working on their warm-up activities, drop in on the reading or writing of one of the students by completing a quick conference or a quick assessment. The warm-up activities are designed to provide quick independent practice. When you have completed your check on one student, call the group together for the intervention instruction planned for that day. The intervention can begin with some of the students taking a few minutes to share their reading and thinking focused by the warm-up cards.

How Else Can You Use This Technique to Accelerate Instruction?

You can adapt the warm-up cards for almost any level, interest, or strategy. You can design them to focus on word-study strategies, comprehension strategies, and even issues related to affective concerns. They can be designed to address the variations even among learners in the same small intervention group. They can be designed to scaffold the levels of understanding in subsequent lessons as well. See Figure 2–9 for some examples of these different types of cards.

e d maximizes the relatively short time he has with his in-class intervention group. By recording and reflecting on his interactions, he has learned that the group members are still struggling with some key word-study strategies. He has designed his warm-up cards to focus students on adding word identification strategies they need. As students are working on their warm-up activities, he quickly invites one of the students to complete an oral reading check with him. He notes a few of the miscues from the assessed student and uses them with the small group to look more closely at using word strategies to figure out or cross-check those words. As students report out on their warm-up tasks, Ed engages them in more responsive instruction based on students' sharing. As he completes his coaching of the group, he quickly notes students' levels of performance and engagement and records a few coaching directions for the next meeting.

Figure 2–8 Intervention Analysis Grid

Intervention Analysis Grid

Directions: As you meet with a classroom-based small group of students for intervention, use this grid to capture the interaction with and performance of the students. Indicate the time you initiated contact, the time instruction started, and the time instruction ended. Place the names of the students across the top of the grid. Identify a target focus for the warm-up activity for each student. Track the interactions between the students and you. Use a plus sign (+) to indicate a positive performance by a student. Use a minus sign (–) to indicate concerns about a student's performance. Use a plus sign to indicate strong engagement by a student. Use a minus sign to indicate concerns about a student's engagement level. Identify a target focus for coaching each student in subsequent meetings of the group.

Time Initiated:			Time Instruction Started:			Time Instruction Ended:	
	Student 1	Student 2	Student 3	Student 4	Student 5	Student 6	General Group Observations
Warm-Up Target							
Number of Interactions with Teacher							
Level of Performance in Interactions							
Level of Engagement in Group							
Target Areas for Coaching Addressed							
Target Areas for Coaching Needed							
Other Observations About Student							

Figure 2–9 Warm-Up Cards

Warm-Up Cards

Directions: Prepare reading warm-up cards (like those below) and strategically disseminate them as students come to the table for intervention work. As students work on their tasks, drop in on them one at a time. Assess oral reading and understanding and scaffold instruction as needed. When all students are ready, invite them to share their tasks in the small group, where you can continue to monitor their competency and confidence and scaffold instruction as needed.

WARM-UP CARDS: Text-to-Self Connections

Reread a favorite part of yours. Be ready to share that part and why it was a favorite.	Find a place where you did some thinking. Be ready to read it to us and tell us about your thinking.
Reread something that surprised you. Be ready to share that part and why it surprised you.	Reread a part that tells about one of the characters. Be ready to read it to us and tell us about the character.
Think about a part that tells how one of the characters is unlike you. Be ready to explain how the two of you are different.	Free choice: Choose a part you want to reread. Be ready to share it with us.

Figure 2–9 *Continued*

Warm-Up Cards

WARM-UP CARDS: Beyond Text-to-Self Connections

Make a connection between one of the characters in this story and another story you have read. Support your idea using information from both books.	Make a connection between something in the setting in this story and another story you have read. Support your idea using information from both books.
Make a connection between one of the characters in this story and a person in the news. Support your idea.	Make a connection between something in the setting in this story and something you know from history. Support your idea.
Make a connection between an important event in this story and another story you have read. Support your idea using information from both books.	Make a connection between an important event in this story and something going on in the news. Support your idea.

WARM-UP CARDS: Word Study

Find a word in the part you read that was at first hard for you but then you figured it out. Be ready to share that word and what your strategy was.	Find a word in the part you read that was at first hard for you but then you used context clues to figure it out. Be ready to share that word and how you used context clues.
Find some words in the part you read that are more interesting ways of saying some overused words. Be ready to share these word choices by the author.	Find some words in the part you read that all share the same root word. Be ready to share those words and show how they are all related.
Find some words in the part you read that all come from the same category of something. Be ready to share those words and show how they are all related.	Find some of the best adjectives used by the author in the part you read. Be ready to share those words.

Picture Walk Alternatives

What Is the Goal?

In small groups, you want to spend most of the relatively short time you have coaching your students as they interact with the text, and you want them to be successful at constructing meaning as they read. Part of achieving that goal relies on effective front-loading for the lesson, but you also don't want front-loading to consume so much of the time that you don't have the time you need for the actual reading and response. The goal is to find a balance between the before, during, and after phases of the small-group lessons. It's also important to be more conscious about whether your front-loading is creating a sense of urgency in your students, making them want to read the text, or whether you are doing so much front-loading that you are actually reducing students' need to read the text.

Why Is the Goal Important?

Front-loading the reading is important if your goal for small groups is successful meaning making. Successful front-loading focuses on five key points. First, make sure students have the background knowledge they need to be able to make sense of the text they'll be reading. Second, if students have background knowledge, focus on activating their schema to help them bring what they already know to the page. Third, address key skills and strategies with the students that they will need to be successful with the text. This is especially important for addressing conceptually difficult vocabulary students will encounter in the text. Fourth, as you front-load, you want to create interest—urgency—in reading the text. Finally, get the readers focused so they have a purpose guiding them while they read.

But in trying to address those five key points, teachers can unknowingly spend too much time getting the students ready for the reading, leaving less time—and, in some cases, less need—for the actual reading. One popular practice for front-loading texts with visual support is taking a picture walk through a book. Unfortunately, it can grow a bit tiresome for some students. It can consume too much time, tire the students, and reveal so much that it actually reduces the urgency to read the text. In light of our concerns about effectively front-loading texts, we need to rethink this typical but tired practice. Alternative instructional techniques could bring better balance to your lessons.

One thing that would help would be to have techniques that you could use at the beginning of small-group instruction that would actually reveal your students' level of background knowledge, including vocabulary needed to be successful with the text. That would help you quickly ascertain how much front-loading you would need to do.

How Can You Evaluate Your Current Efforts in Meeting This Goal?

To gain a sense of how you are doing with your balance in front-loading the text versus coaching your students while they read the text, you can return to recording your small-group sessions, shifting your focus to the proportion of time you are spending on each aspect of instruction. In the initial recordings, simply record the time devoted to the front-loading and the time related to coaching while reading and responding. Monitor that so you can shift the balance in a manner that helps you make more effective use of your time. Keep in mind that a shift in and of itself is only desirable if your students can maintain their comprehension. Jeopardizing meaning making by reducing front-loading is not the end goal, so for each session you also need to consider the level of understanding the students demonstrate during that lesson.

What Can You Use to Make Progress in Meeting This Goal?

Use front-loading activities that actually let you follow the lead of your students in determining how much explicit instruction they need in developing background knowledge. Oczkus (2004) suggested three activities that you could use at the start of your lessons to assess what background knowledge and language students are bringing to a topic or a text:

1. **Word Prediction Technique:** Pass out a few sticky notes to each student and identify the theme or topic of the text you will read by writing it on your sticky note. Put this note in the center of the table or board in your small-group reading area. Then ask the students to write on each of their sticky notes a word they predict will be in the text based on that topic. Ask students to reveal their words and talk about why they think they might be in the reading. As they reveal their words, you can start to make a word web on the table, moving your notes around to show how they are connected to one another. Based on the knowledge and language revealed by your students as they share their predictions and organize your web, you can assess whether they have enough background and vocabulary to move into the text. You can come to the table with a few key

words from the text already written on your sticky notes and share those with the students and integrate them into the web if additional word work is needed.

2. **One-Minute Book Look:** Give students one minute to walk themselves through the book. Say, "Flip, do not rip, your way through the book and when one minute is finished, I want you to put your finger on your favorite picture that you saw in the book." As they make their way through the book, drop in on spontaneous conversations. Once the minute is up, call on students to start sharing their favorite pictures. Again you can authentically assess the background knowledge and vocabulary they bring to the reading from listening and probing carefully as they describe their favorite pages. Be prepared to point out a few other critical pages or words if more front-loading seems necessary.

3. **I Know–I Don't Know Graphic Organizer:** Using this organizer, invite your students to do a quick scan of the text—another one-minute flip, not rip. When the minute is done, they should be prepared to tell you one thing they already know about the topic and one thing they don't know about the topic (see Figure 2–10). They can write their ideas on scrap paper or on the graphic organizer and at the end of the minute, they can share their revelations. Record these on a chart you have prepared. As described before, you can assess the background knowledge and vocabulary they bring to the reading from listening and probing carefully as they describe their discoveries. Be prepared to point out a few other critical insights and ideas and add them to the chart if more front-loading seems necessary.

How Else Can You Use This Technique to Accelerate Instruction?

Another alternative to the picture walk that may have more power for readers as they encounter texts with less picture support is a *text walk*. A text walk actively involves the students in discovering the organization of the text while they create a graphic organizer to guide them as they read the text. You can guide your students to move through the text, looking for indicators like boldface headers. As students discover boldface headers, they can place them on their own webs or grids, leaving space to record interesting details and important information when they read those sections (see Figure 2–11).

By rotating these and similar activities into your repertoire of front-loading activities for small groups, you'll help students get familiar with a number of techniques that you will use to tighten up your large-group lessons. For example, the word prediction technique in the large group allows even more vocabulary to surface. As the words are revealed, students can record them in a grid that they cut apart to develop their own word webs.

ed has selected an informational text on wolves to use for his small group. He has looked through the text and identified key topical vocabulary with which he thinks his students might have difficulty. When they come to the table, he passes out sticky notes and invites each student to predict one word that he or she thinks would be in a book about wolves. As his students reveal their answers, Ed probes to ask why they think that word might be in the book. They look for connections across their words as they talk about wolves. Ed can sense that some additional preparation will be needed for the students to be successful with the text. He grabs a few more of the word cards he has prepared and introduces them to the students. They discuss how to connect them with the words they have predicted. He is happy when students identify some of those words as they work through the text together and that they spend most of their time focused on the text and not just on the front-loading activities.

Figure 2–10 I Know–I Don't Know Graphic Organizer

I Know–I Don't Know Graphic Organizer

I Know	I Don't Know

Figure 2–11 Text Walk Information Organizer

Text Walk Information Organizer

Boldface Header	Important Ideas	Interesting Details

Word Count Boosters

What Is the Goal?

The bottom line in the use of small groups is to accelerate the instruction for those students who need more than an academic year's worth of growth in an academic year's worth of time. Teachers need to work to close the performance gap between the readers in their classes and expected proficiency levels. While we can get excited about any progress our students make, we need to temper our excitement if that progress still leaves a learner short of expected proficiency levels. Practice is important to help students not only make progress but become proficient. The goal is to intentionally plan practice opportunities in small groups in such a manner that they will impact all readers, especially those who need assistance the most.

Why Is the Goal Important?

Practice—actual time spent reading—is critical for improvement (Allington 1983) and often separates more proficient readers from those who are less so (Stanovich 1986). The practice gap actually increases the performance gap, especially as students get older. Those who are more proficient continue to practice and grow as readers. At the same time, those who are less proficient often resist and withdraw from additional practice and stall their growth.

We have had two aha moments recently when looking at practice. When presenting a workshop on flexible grouping, we heard a participant vigorously defend her school's decision to guarantee that every child would read appropriate-level text for thirty minutes each day. The school had taken great pains to reorganize the school day so that children could move to their appropriate reading groups and work with teachers during that thirty-minute block. We pointed out, however, that while the effort to guarantee that every child received at least thirty minutes of small-group instruction with appropriate texts was important, one also needs to consider what happens to each child during the balance of the day. There were over six hours left in the student's school day and if practice issues were not addressed in the instructional decisions for the remainder of the school day, it would be very likely that those in need of the most practice would not get it (Glasswell and Ford 2011). Unfortunately, when we stopped and looked at our own practices, we saw that sometimes those readers with the greatest needs were not receiving the amount of practice they really needed. If our whole-class texts are above their levels, for example, the texts don't provide much opportunity for practice. If our collection of accessible texts for use during independent reading time are within their range, they might provide valuable practice, but it is without supervision. That really means we must make sure the practice students receive during small-group time is as intensive as possible. If, during that time, the texts we select for our students with the greatest needs actually provide fewer words, pages, and time for practice, we need to rethink those methods.

The second critical insight came when we thought about the reading mileage of our students. More advanced readers commonly process more words because they read longer and denser texts, and they do it faster (Glasswell and Ford 2011). One day in the classroom, we were working with readers in need of the greatest support. We used a sixteen-page level G text that contained about eighty words in the entire book (five of which were multisyllabic). Then we moved to a little stronger group that was reading at the N level. For them we had selected the first chapter of ten pages from an easy chapter book. This chapter had eighty-seven words on the first page alone, and eleven of them were multisyllabic! By the time the kids in the N group had read the whole chapter, they had received more than ten times as much practice as the students in the other group with greater needs. That aha moment caused us to want to study the amount of practice we are providing students with the texts we are using during small groups. We need to measure the amount of print our students are reading. We should take note of the word count for each text that we bring to the table. We need to stay aware of discrepancies in the quantity of practice students are receiving at different levels and think about what steps we can take to provide comparable amounts of practice with text for each group.

How Can You Evaluate Your Current Efforts in Meeting This Goal?

You need to look both at the way your small-group work fits into your overall use of different grouping arrangements as well as look at the quality of the small groups in and of themselves. You can use the Profile of Instruction Based on Groups of Students and Access to Text to examine the proportion of your instructional time devoted to small-group work (see Figure 2–12). Increasing the use of small groups allows more opportunities to effectively target instruction and provide supervised practice, especially for those who need it the most. In analyzing your school day, account for the amount of time you teach using whole groups, using small groups, and engaging students in independent work. Reflect on whether those allotments are appropriate in terms of the needs of your students.

Once you have adjusted those allotments to better meet the needs of instruction in your class, look more closely at the time and frequency with which you meet with small groups. Remember, equal is not necessarily the best way to judge your use of small groups. You want to provide as much support as possible for all students but especially for those who need your help the most. At any level of reading, students can benefit from interaction with you. As we have discovered by using other instructional accelerators, we can strengthen the thinking, vocabulary, strategy use, and social interaction techniques of the most proficient readers and those that need our help the most. You can guide some groups more indirectly while you guide other groups more directly. When directly guiding groups, be intentional about providing supervised practice.

What Can You Use to Make Progress in Meeting This Goal?

There are several ways to boost the word counts students are exposed to. The first thing to work on is text selection. When teachers match a text for a small group, they often consider the level at which the students have been assessed. However, even books that are identified as being at the same level have a lot of variation in terms of their word count. When you select a text especially for your readers in need of more support, choose one that can maximize practice opportunities with a high word count. You can record this information on the Practice Tally (Word Counts in Small Groups) sheet (see Figure 2–13).

Another way to provide more practice is to read shorter texts more than once. You can double the word count of a reading experience by revisiting a book, but you need to think about how to do that in ways that will excite, not bore, your students. If reading is equated to boredom, you will struggle hard to keep your readers in need of the most practice engaged in the most practice. There are a number of interesting ways to reread texts. One of the most effective activities is to set up an informal readers theatre for a narrative story with multiple characters and lots of dialogue. We divide up the character parts in a story with dialogue, sometimes assigning each student a part and sometimes having more than one student read together on a part. We allow a little time for the students to practice their parts (providing additional practice) and then reread the text as a readers theatre performance right at the table. With a really good story, the students sometimes ask to perform it for the class or even for other classes, so we encourage them to practice together during their independent work time—rereading again—so they will have a polished performance to take public (providing yet even more practice!).

You can also increase the amount of practice for a group by selecting more than one text to use during small-group time. Two related texts will provide additional texts, pages, and words to practice. Topically related texts often can be set up with the same front-loading activities (imagine two books about snakes) but will contain slightly different information and vocabulary. Then you get two texts with one front-loading preview, helping the balance you needed to work on as well. Assign some students to each text and then have them switch after an initial discussion to give additional practice to all students in the group.

How Else Can You Use This Technique to Accelerate Instruction?

One way you can use the insights mentioned in the previous section to accelerate instruction is to help your readers discover the value in reading series. Series are often formulaic and written at similar levels of difficulty, but each book in the series is slightly different (Opitz, Ford, with Zbaracki 2006). Once you introduce students to a series (which you can intentionally do at first through read-alouds and then by having students read them when in small groups), students will be able to take what they know about the first book and immediately use it to negotiate subsequent books in the series. Having readers move through a series is an effective way to provide needed practice without having to provide a lot of external motivation. Conceivably, readers should be able to read through familiar series books more quickly than they would unrelated books, so they will likely read more books within the year.

Since Ed had some critical insights about practice and the need to provide more time, pages, and words for his students with the greatest needs, he first altered the frequency with which he meets with his small groups. While he sees the students in each of his groups at least a couple of times each week, he sees those in need of the greatest help twice as often, doubling his contact with them. Whenever he selects a text to use with those groups, he is more intentional than he used to be. In looking at leveled readers, he almost always chooses books with greater word counts to increase the number of pages and words he can place in front of the readers in those groups. He has added a number of rereading techniques to intensify practice. His students are now asking him if they can divide the story into parts and perform it for the rest of the class. This has turned them on to series with relatable characters and lots of dialogue, and they've become fast friends with Alvin Ho, Raymond and Graham, and George Brown. They have turned informational books into newscasts, dividing up the content and rehearsing parts before sharing information with others, interviewing famous people, and providing lists of helpful tips.

Profile of Instruction Based on Groups of Students and Access to Text

Instructional Routine (Number of Minutes Devoted to . . .)	Below-Level Readers	At-Level Readers	Above-Level Readers
Large-Group Instruction			
Small-Group Instruction			
Independent Work			
Total Minutes			

Figure 2–13 Practice Tally (Word Counts in Small Groups)

Practice Tally (Word Counts in Small Groups)

	Group _____	Group _____	Group _____
Selected Text(s)			
Word Count(s) of Selected Text(s)			
Number of Times Repeated			
Total Practice			

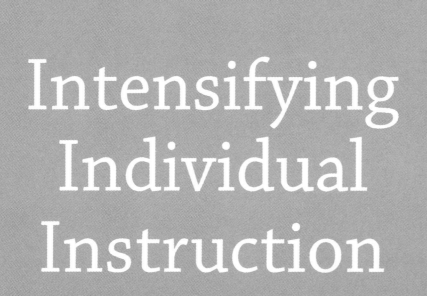

Intensifying
Individual
Instruction

3

There's no such thing as a kid

who hates reading. There are kids who love reading,

and kids who are reading the wrong books.

JAMES PATTERSON

Iiteracy coach Brenda talks with Kemmery about the classroom independent silent
reading block she has just observed and begins by asking, "So how do you think
it went?"

Without hesitation, Kemmery comments, "I was pleased with how engaged the
students seemed to be with their texts but thought some must have been pretending.
I mean, there is no way that they could read with the kind of speed their page-turning
indicated. And sure enough, when I probed individual students to see what they com-
prehended, their responses indicated that they hadn't! I want to use this independent
time to accelerate their reading growth but now I'm wondering if that can happen,
especially if they aren't comprehending."

Brenda probes a bit further. "So what do you think was going on?"

Kemmery thinks aloud with Brenda. "I think it shows that the students know
what silent reading is supposed to look like on the outside when I tell them to read independently, but I am beginning to wonder if all know how silent reading works inside
their heads. Do they know what readers really do when they read silently? I know I
have never really taught them that. I guess I have just expected them to do it."

"You might be onto something, Kemmery. How do you think you could discover
if your hunch is right?"

"I know I can begin by assessing them. I can talk with individual students to get
their thoughts about what they think silent reading means. But I'm not sure what I will
do with what I discover. I mean, how do you teach silent reading? It's such a covert
activity! I'm not sure where to begin."

Why Is It Important to Strengthen Individual Instruction?

If an instructional program is to lead to accelerated growth for learners with the greatest needs, the independent learning experiences students encounter—including independent silent reading—need to be examined to make sure that students are gaining the most from them. We (Ford and Opitz 2002) have previously argued that the power of instruction away from the teacher needs to rival the power of instruction with the teacher. Independent work needs to be intentionally planned around meaningful reading and writing practice opportunities. Fortunately, many teachers are discovering systems that help teach students to grow in their urgency, stamina, and self-regulation, sustaining productive practice independently (Boushey and Moser 2014).

Sometimes productive independent work may flow from whole-class and small-group instruction, such as in those models we describe in the first two sections of this book (grouping without tracking, jigsawing, and connected literature circles). It also is more possible when using individualized instructional models such as a focused readers workshop (Opitz and Ford 2008) or the supportive workshop approach implemented in the School Enrichment Model for Reading (SEM-R), by Sally Reis (2009) and her colleagues. Reis' concerns grew out of an observed pattern of talented readers selecting relatively easy texts in independent reading programs. Unfortunately, that often meant even talented readers resisted or withdrew from reading when faced with more complex, challenging texts. Did the expectation that all texts should be easy grow from independent programs that fell short of challenging readers? Reis argued for a more supportive workshop model in which choice was not wide open but supported by the teacher, leading to more appropriate texts getting in the hands of more readers. Conferring with readers becomes more intentional as well to help readers work through instead of resist challenging problems within the texts. Even though they were focusing on talented readers when implementing the program, Reis and her colleagues (2011) were able to show that the supportive model actually raised the performance of learners across levels.

We are afraid that without greater teacher attention, independent approaches in classrooms with diverse levels of readers might actually widen gaps. We observed classrooms in which students differed significantly in their levels of engagement during independent reading time. This often translated to gaps in the amount of actual practice different students gained from those experiences. In addition, with wide-open choice, students differed in the quality of reading experiences during this time. In one third-grade classroom, we remember watching one student plow through the first book in the Inheritance fantasy series *Eragon* while another student reread one of the Berenstain Bears books. This issue has caused some experts (e.g., Routman 2003) to discuss how teachers need to tighten up recreational independent reading programs and think about how they can help accomplish instructional outcomes. Routman suggests tightening the teacher guidance of book selection by students, increasing the time set aside for all readers, monitoring for meaning making, and systematizing conferences, including goal setting between student and teacher.

In our previous work focused on organizational structures teachers can use to enhance learning away from the teacher, we thoroughly discussed how teachers can use learning centers for this type of work (Ford and Opitz 2002). But we also proposed alternative formats that teachers can use to engage students with meaningful independent projects. What we said then holds true for what we propose here. But here we zoom in on how to use reading—silent reading in particular—as probably one of the most valuable individual work options students can and should be doing. Without a doubt, there is ample evidence to support what seems like common sense: students who read more are better readers (see Allington 2008 for a review of several research findings as well as Krashen 1993). And if we know students need to do more reading because they benefit from it, then struggling readers may need even more time to practice if we are going to accelerate their growth. Like any other activity that we want to perfect, meaningful practice matters. Yet what we often discover in our visits to classrooms is that when children are expected to work independently, reading is sometimes left out of the individual work activities. And when it is left in, it often falls short.

Five Classroom Catalysts for Intensifying Individual Instruction

In this section, we present five classroom catalysts for accelerating the growth of all learners in addressing key issues related to engaging students in independent work, especially individual silent reading opportunities:

1. Silent reading assessments
2. Text selection guidelines for silent reading

3. Stamina-building activities

4. Reading out loud with partners

5. Text response activities

In regard to intensifying student independent work, especially individual silent reading, we start with assessment tools to assist teachers in knowing what students' ideas and perceptions are regarding silent reading. Then we move to strategies to improve student text selection for silent reading opportunities. With the right text, we can then turn our attention to staying with the texts by looking at stamina builders. We shift focus to productive social interaction and support structures in strengthening activities when students read to someone else and work with study buddies. Finally, we look at ways students can go deeper with their texts by intensifying response activities.

Each of these catalysts is illustrated with classroom examples and/or appropriate support materials and each is framed around five questions:

1. What is the goal?

2. Why is the goal important?

3. How can you evaluate your current efforts in meeting this goal?

4. What can you use to make progress in meeting this goal?

5. How else can you use this technique to accelerate instruction?

Independent work, including individual silent reading, is a process that needs to be supported at all phases. Efforts might begin by examining which parts of the process are in need of the greatest support—assessment, text selection, sustained effort, working with buddies, or responding to texts. While we can focus on one aspect of independent work including silent reading, we can intensify instruction more powerfully when we can connect these ideas to strengthen support throughout the process. These ideas are designed to initially help you move from teacher-directed support for independent work to student-driven independent work, where students take responsibility for their levels of engagement. Look at the ideas as interrelated techniques to tighten up the part of your program dedicated to independent work. Instructional acceleration requires the teacher to have tools to capture, analyze, and improve the levels of engagement of students in individual instructional settings. Instructional acceleration occurs when the teacher uses techniques like these and eventually transfers the responsibility to the students to operate effectively by themselves.

In discussing various aspects of independent work including individual silent reading with especially young children, we have discovered that a number of picture books can be great springboards for those discussions. In Figure 3–1, we have identified books that can support discussions about the importance of finding the right book for the right reader, strategies to use in choosing a good book, the need for stamina and practice, purposes for reading, and reasons for reading to others.

Figure 3–1 Books to Support Independent Reading

Books for Discussing the Importance of Finding the Right Book for the Right Reader

The Best Book to Read, by Debbie Bertram and Susan Bloom (New York: Random House, 2008)

The Lonely Book, by Kate Bernheimer (New York: Schwartz and Wade Books, 2012)

Have I Got a Book for You, by Melanie Watt (Tonawanda, NY: Kids Can Press, 2009)

Read Anything Good Lately? by Susan Allan and Jane Lindaman (Minneapolis: Millbrook, 2003)

The Book That I Love to Read, by Joe Fitzpatrick (Oakville, ON: Flowerpot Press, 2010)

Miss Marlarkey Leaves No Reader Behind, by Judy Finchler and Kevin O'Malley (New York: Walker, 2006)

I Like Books, by Anthony Browne (New York: Walker, 2003)

Wild About Books, by Judy Sierra (New York: Alfred A. Knopf, 2004)

Books for Discussing Strategies for Students to Use in Choosing a Good Book on Their Own

Goldie Socks and the Three Libearians, by Jackie Mims Hopkins (Fort Atkinson, WI: Upstart Books, 2007)

Books for Discussing the Importance of Stamina and Practice While Reading Independently

Excuse Me, I'm Trying to Read, by Mary Jo Amani (Watertown, MA: Charlesbridge, 2012)

I Hate Reading: How to Get Through 20 Minutes of Reading a Day Without Really Reading, by Arthur and Henry Bacon (Fort Atkinson, WI: Upstart Books, 2008)

I Don't Like to Read, by Nancy Carlson (New York: Viking, 2007)

Hooray for Reading Day, by Margery Cuyler (New York: Scholastic, 2008)

Read to Tiger, by S. J. Fore (New York: Scholastic, 2010)

How to Teach a Slug to Read, by Susan Pearson (New York: Scholastic, 2011)

continues

Figure 3–1 *Continued*

Books for Discussing Purposes for Reading

The Incredible Book Eating Boy, by Oliver Jeffers (New York: Philomel, 2006)

Born to Read, by Judy Sierra (New York: Alfred A. Knopf, 2008)

Reading Makes You Feel Good, by Todd Parr (New York: Little, Brown, 2005)

Book! Book! Book! by Deborah Bruss (New York: Scholastic, 2001)

Henry and the Buccaneer Bunnies, by Carolyn Crimi (Somerville, MA: Candlewick, 2005)

The Wonderful Book, by Leonid Gore (New York: Scholastic, 2010)

Dear Mr. Blueberry, by Simon James (New York: McElderry Books, 1991)

Wolves, by Emily Gravett (New York: Simon and Schuster, 2006)

Souperchicken, by MaryJane Auch and Herm Auch (New York: Holiday House, 2003)

Me . . . Jane, by Patrick McDonnell (New York: Little, Brown, 2011)

A Library for Juana, by Pat Mora (New York: Alfred A. Knopf, 2002)

Books for Discussing Reasons for Reading to Others

The Best Time to Read, by Debbie Bertram and Susan Bloom (New York: Random House, 2005)

I Will Not Read This Book, by Cece Meng (New York: Clarion, 2011)

The Little "Read" Hen, by Dianne de Las Casas (Gretna, LA: Pelican, 2013)

Alfred Zector: Book Collector, by Kelly DiPucchio (New York: Harper, 2010)

Miss Smith's Incredible Storybook, by Michael Garland (New York: Dutton Children's Books, 2003)

Miss Smith Reads Again, by Michael Garland (New York: Dutton Children's Books, 2006)

ZooZical, by Judy Sierra (New York: Alfred A. Knopf, 2011)

Poetry Anthologies with Verses Celebrating All Aspects of Reading

The Bookworm's Feast: A Potluck of Poems, by J. Patrick Lewis (New York: Dial, 1999)

Bookspeak: Poems About Books, by Laura Purdie Salas (New York: Clarion, 2011)

I Am the Book, by Lee Bennett Hopkins (New York: Holiday House, 2011)

Good Books, Good Times, by Lee Bennett Hopkins (New York: Harper Collins, 2000)

Silent Reading Assessments

What Is the Goal?

The goal is to make sure that all students are engaged during independent silent reading opportunities. To that end, you'll need to find out if all students understand what it means to read silently. You'll also want to know what they select to read and how they approach independent silent reading.

Why Is the Goal Important?

Independent work structures are just one more way of grouping students and managing your literacy block. If you have tightened your large- and small-group instruction, you need to tighten your individual work opportunities as well. Making sure that this independent time is used as effectively as any other instructional time throughout the day is important. If you are going to target instruction in small groups and in conferences with individuals, your other students will need to be engaged in productive work on their own. You need to feel confident that your students will be able to productively engage in activities like independent silent reading.

How Can You Evaluate Your Current Efforts in Meeting This Goal?

Although independent silent reading (i.e., scheduled time when students select their own texts and independently read them without interruption) is important, teachers are sometimes reluctant to have students engage with it. One reason for their reluctance centers on the challenge of determining whether students are really reading during this time. Their concern is often fueled by an emphasis on accountability in their school and the fact that they must show evidence of growth on nearly every activity their students perform. If you feel this pressure, remember that independent silent reading is a time for students to practice without penalty. You can provide evidence of their growth later when you use one of the many other assessments you have available to capture their performance and proficiency levels. However, you can build in some accountability to tighten up the use of this time to relieve some of your concern. For example, once the silent reading time is finished, students can engage in conversations with others about what they have read and make comments in reading journals. They can also record what they have read, including the date, title, and a brief evaluation of the text or something they learned by reading the text, using an Independent Silent Reading Log (see Figure 3–2). Finally, you can use your own log to record what you observe when they are reading and make notes for yourself (see Figure 3–3).

But even after you tighten up your independent silent reading opportunities, some students will still resist silent reading. One of our students expressed this resistance when he said upon being asked to read silently, "I don't like to do that. Let's wait and do it tomorrow." We have a hunch that this reticence is due, in part, to students' lack of understanding about what silent reading is. It reminded us of the advice the two twelve-year-old authors Henry and Arthur Bacon give in their book for children, *I Hate Reading: How to Get Through 20 Minutes of Reading a Day Without Really Reading* (2008): "Look at the book and move your eyes from side to side. Slowly. Eyes on book" (2). We wonder if that is what students think silent reading is. Do they know what exactly they are supposed to do? Teaching children how to read silently is far different from expecting them to engage with it. Perhaps you have focused on reasons to read silently and behaviors you should see when kids are reading silently (staying in one place, sitting quietly, etc.). Perhaps you have even given them license to read in certain ways, allowing for some developmental differences (read the words or read the pictures). But do they really know what should be going on inside their heads? You can use the student Silent Reading Interview Guide (see Figure 3–4) as one way to ascertain your children's understanding of what silent reading entails. Hearing what students think about independent silent reading is a good starting place for you to clear up any misconceptions and to inform your thinking about teaching students *how* to read silently.

What Can You Use to Make Progress in Meeting This Goal?

You can use student records of their independent silent reading to take note of the kinds of texts they are reading and what they are thinking about them. You can also conference with students about their texts and make note of what they discuss. Their comments will shed light on the degree of their ability to read silently with comprehension. When analyzing student responses to the questions you pose on the student interview guide, look for any misconceptions that might occur and design lessons to help students replace these misconceptions with more accurate views of silent reading. For example, if student responses indicate that they do not know what they are supposed to do when reading silently, especially the covert activities that happen inside their heads, you can use think-alouds to model your own covert behaviors.

There are three additional ways that you can use the results of silent reading assessments to accelerate instruction. They are as follows:

- Remind students that silent reading is a little more time-efficient than oral reading because they do not have to pronounce and articulate every word. Consequently, students should be able to read more texts, thereby seeing more words per reading session and accelerating their reading growth.
- As with other lessons to help students better understand how to read silently, you can use the think-aloud to model your own process when reading silently and orally and point out the differences to students.
- To further help students understand the differences between oral and silent reading, use a lesson that incorporates a strategy called rapid retrieval of information (Opitz and Rasinski 2008) because students will first read silently and then read orally. To do so, use four main teaching procedures:

  1. Provide students with individual copies of a text to read and make sure to provide time for them to read them silently.
  2. Once all have had time to read silently, present individual students with tasks such as reading aloud a sentence that explains a character trait, a sentence that verifies a given point, or a phrase that explains a word.
  3. Once you provide students with their specific task, ask them to reread their texts in search of information they can use to complete the task.
  4. Then ask students to read aloud their discoveries.

Kemmery uses the activities in this section to ascertain her students' understanding of silent reading and to teach them different aspects of silent reading and how to get the most from independent reading. In one lesson she begins with a familiar big book, reading it aloud and inviting students to chime in when they would like. Once finished, she comments, "That was fun reading! I could hear nearly every one of you using your voice in just the right way to convey the meaning of the text. You are such good readers!"

Having stated what they know how to do, she uses what they know to teach them something they need to know, saying, "As good as your oral reading is, there is another type of reading that readers do when they read in and out of school. You have probably seen your parents do this kind of reading and other people, too. I'm going to do this kind of reading right now, and I want you tell me what you see and hear."

She selects another familiar big book and displays it for all to see. She reads a few pages silently to herself as they watch and then stops and asks, "So what did you see me doing?"

Rory comments, "It looked like you were moving your eyes when you were looking at the words."

Annabelle adds, "I also noticed that you pointed to the words but you didn't say them out loud. I didn't hear anything."

"You two are good observers! I did just what you said. What I was doing when I was looking at the words was reading them in my mind. I was reading them to myself. But just like when I read aloud, I had to do more than just look at the words. I had to make sense of what they words were saying. Reading always has to make sense. This kind of reading is called *silent reading* because nobody can hear what you are reading. And that's what you are going to do when you read independently today."

Figure 3–2 Independent Silent Reading Log

Independent Silent Reading Log

Name: _____

Date	Reading Material	Overall Response

Figure 3–3 Teacher Observation of Independent Silent Reading

Teacher Observation of Independent Silent Reading

Directions: Write the date, name of student, and the text you observe them reading in the appropriate columns. Write any pertinent notes to record what you observed when watching the student read. Observations might include reading behaviors such as how the student actually read the material (no sound, whispering, orally to self, and lip movements).

Date	Student	Reading Material	Observations

Figure 3–4 Silent Reading Interview Guide

Silent Reading Interview Guide

Your Name: _____ **Date:** _____ **Group:** _____

1. When someone tells you to read silently, what do you think you are supposed to do?

2. What do you actually do when you are reading silently? What happens inside your head that nobody can hear?

3. How is silent reading different from oral reading?

4. Do you like to read silently? Why or why not?

Text Selection Guidelines for Silent Reading

What Is the Goal?

We want students to understand how to select appropriate texts for silent reading and what silent reading entails.

Why Is the Goal Important?

Providing time for students to read silently enables them to develop the ability to have their eyes move ahead of the text, allowing them to read without hesitation. In Betts' words, "the individual develops a desirable eye-voice span" (1946, 385). In addition to fluency, silent reading fosters other important reading skills such as increased vocabulary growth (Anderson 1996) and comprehension (Linehart, Zigmond, and Cooley 1981; Reutzel and Hollingsworth 1991; Guthrie et al. 1999).

How Can You Evaluate Your Current Efforts in Meeting This Goal?

You can use students' individual reading logs to see what kinds of choices they are making. You can also observe students to see how much time they are using to select versus read texts. They should be spending the majority of their time on reading rather than selecting.

What Can You Use to Make Progress in Meeting This Goal?

You want students to choose texts at an appropriate level, in this case texts they will be able to read with ease. To get all students engaged in silent reading, you need to establish some text selection guidelines for and with your students. Following are four ways to teach children how to select texts:

Techniques	Explanation
1. Have a whole-class meeting and encourage students to generate text selection criteria.	Involving students in determining the criteria helps them better understand what it is they need to look for. Once the class has generated a list, post it in the room and encourage students to refer to it when they are selecting texts.
2. Explain to students how to use the thumb test: • Open the book to the middle. • Open up your right or left hand. • Read a page of the book to yourself. • Put one finger down every time you come to a word you don't know, starting with your pinky and ending with your thumb. • If you finish the page and your thumb is still up, you probably have a text that is good for you. If you have all or most fingers up, you probably have a text that will be very easy for you to read. You can either keep this text or look for another one that will be a little more challenging.	This test has been around for quite some time (Veatch 1968) and has proven helpful for many students, so you can be confident using it with your students, too.
3. Provide children with a list of questions about the texts they are considering reading.	Use the questions in Figure 3–5 to help your students become more insightful about selecting texts.
4. Read aloud parts of different texts.	By reading aloud many different kinds of texts, you can help children see that there are many good texts aside from those they may consider all-time favorites.

Some children will reread familiar texts during independent silent reading time, which is valuable too. Through this practice, they can gain much in the way of developing a sight-word vocabulary and other reading skills. Besides, doing so is just plain fun!

How Else Can You Use This Technique to Accelerate Instruction?

Finding the right book for the right student is the key for accelerating growth during independent silent reading. You can start by sharing any of a number of books written for children that discuss the need for the readers to find the right book and some that actually discuss strategies children can use for choosing (see Figure 3–1). Since many students may not know all the options that are out there (it's hard enough for teachers to keep up with all the great texts being published for kids!), text selection often begins with us knowing what to put in their hands first (and second and third . . .) until they can take over the process.

Kemmery's literacy coach Brenda suggested three ideas to choose from to get the first books into students' hands. First, she shared an idea their colleague Linda used with her students. Linda saved old book club order forms, and during the first week of school, she passed out a few of them to each student. She invited each student to look closely at the books and then circle three they thought they might want to order. When she initially conferred with each student, she talked with the child about those choices. As a veteran teacher, Linda had an ample classroom collection and she could often place one of those books in the hands of the student. If she did not have any of the books in her room, she often could find one in the school collection. Brenda reminded Kemmery that following a book club—even if you don't order from it—is a good way to know what is new and popular with students.

Brenda shared another idea she had seen teachers use. It was called a *text lineage* (Tatum 2009). More simply, kids were asked to visually represent three or four important books from their lives. You could give each of your students a four-box grid and ask them to draw or write a little about each of the books in the boxes. One teacher had even found an online tool, http://blogs.slj .com/neverendingsearch/2013/06/20/recording-kids-history-as-readers/, that allowed students to build a time line for these important books. The text lineage not only reveals insights into an individual student's view of reading but also helps students make new connections by seeing how their classmates have connected texts.

Brenda pointed out that this is similar to what some have called *reading ladders* (Lesesne 2010). These are available lists (e.g., www.clayton.k12.mo.us

/Page/10141) that help a teacher make suggestions for moving a student from one text to the next: "If you liked this book, you might also like. . . ." Brenda reminded Kemmery that many text archival sites that students can use will also do the same. (See Cooperative Children's Book Center [CCBC] at University of Wisconsin–Madison, where you can search any topic by grade-level recommendations: http://ccbc.education.wisc.edu/.) She showed how teachers can create their own reading ladders to help students make their next selections by thinking about three key things when conferring with the students and looking at what they have read so far (Sibberson 2013):

1. Can you recommend a different version of a book the student has already enjoyed? Can you recommend another book based on the nonfiction topics of the books the student has previously read?
2. Can you recommend another book by an author the student has previously enjoyed or a book by a similar author?
3. Can you recommend a book with a similar format to a book previously enjoyed by the student?

Usually one of these three key questions will lead to a recommendation to keep the student's independent silent reading moving forward.

after thinking through her many options, Kemmery decides to generate a list of text selection criteria with her students. She places the list on a chart large enough for all to see. Knowing that students will need some guided practice when using the list to become most comfortable with it, she provides some small-group reading time on the same day, when each student can select five texts to put into his or her reading basket. The main objective for all reading groups this particular day is to practice making text selections. She falls into a familiar routine for each group as she engages with it. First, she reviews the list of criteria with the students. She then has them use the list while each of them selects five texts from the classroom library for his or her book basket. She provides assistance as needed. Third, she has each choose one to silently read. Doing so enables her to use instructional time as wisely as possible. That is, the students who finish selecting texts before others use their remaining time to read while those who need some additional help from her receive it.

Figure 3–5 Questions to Help Readers Choose Texts

Questions for Readers

Easy Texts

Ask yourself these questions. If you circle YES when answering all three questions, this text is probably an easy one for you.

1. Have you read it before?	Yes	No
2. Can you read it without stumbling?	Yes	No
3. Can you tell the ideas to someone else?	Yes	No

Just-Right Texts

Ask yourself these questions. If you circle YES for most of these questions, this text is probably just right for you.

1. Have you read it before?	Yes	No
2. Can you read most words?	Yes	No
3. Can you tell the ideas to someone else?	Yes	No
4. Could you read this text if you had a little help?	Yes	No

Challenging Texts

Ask yourself these questions. If you circle NO to questions 1 and 2 and YES to questions 3 and 4, this text is probably going to be a little difficult for you.

1. Have you read it before?	Yes	No
2. Can you read most words?	Yes	No
3. Does the text confuse you?	Yes	No
4. Would you need a lot of help to read it?	Yes	No

Stamina-Building Activities

What Is the Goal?

You want students to build their stamina for reading many different types of text. Stamina is a big part of being a successful reader, and it develops over time.

Why Is the Goal Important?

Some students are best at practicing avoidance behaviors when it comes to reading. Their avoidance behaviors take away valuable time that would be better spent building the necessary stamina that reading requires. Stamina develops over time and is important because it enables readers to stay mentally alert for longer periods of time and, therefore, acquire and comprehend a larger reading vocabulary.

How Can You Evaluate Your Current Efforts in Meeting This Goal?

Independent silent reading carries much responsibility, not to mention structure. It is anything but a free-for-all in which students are allowed to do whatever they want. It is a deliberate, planned time of the day with a definite purpose. As students read, you need to make observations of students and make notes about what you see. At other times, you need to keep students focused on reading to help them build stamina. At still other times, you need to help students read their self-selected texts. You can provide this scaffolding in a couple of ways. You might sit with an individual student and read parts of the text in unison. Another way you might help students is to model how to read a part of the text, stop, and summarize what has just been read before reading further. Both of these ways help students further develop stamina by keeping them engaged with reading rather than shutting down because they perceive the text to be too difficult.

You can also use what you know about your students to create individual text baskets for them and have them choose from their baskets. Your choosing will narrow their choices but will ultimately still leave them with some autonomy because they will choose from among the texts that are in their baskets.

When you conduct a whole-class silent reading session, observe students and make notations about how individual students are performing and the amount of time they spend reading. You can make notes for yourself on the Teacher Observation of Independent Silent Reading form (Figure 3–3).

What Can You Use to Make Progress in Meeting This Goal?

As with other classroom procedures you use, having your students know exactly what you expect of them during silent reading is important. Select texts that offer a springboard to discussions about why practice is important and why building their stamina will help them practice (see Figure 3–1). These discussions can help you generate guidelines with students and then post on a poster large enough for all to see as a reminder of what to do when reading independently. This is the type of list that we have generated with former students:

Rules for Independent Silent Reading

- You must read some type of text such as a book, magazine, or comic book.
- If you select something that you don't like, stop reading it and choose something else to read. Remember that you are trying to stay reading the entire reading time.
- You can read a text more than one time if you want.
- You need to keep a list of everything you read during independent reading time, even if you do not finish it. Use the form in your independent reading folder.
- Read the entire reading time and read as much as you can.

Remember that building stamina also allows exposing students to varied texts and genres. You can be very deliberate about having students read different texts and providing time for them to engage with these different texts. Because there is interplay among the reader, the text, and the context, make sure to provide reading time in all content areas and gradually expect students to read more of their content-area texts independently.

How Else Can You Use This Technique to Accelerate Instruction?

As you see students' engagement with texts grow, increase the amount of time you expect them to read independently. This time will fluctuate depending on the type of text they are reading and the amount of interest they have in it. Providing all students with in-school time to read is essential if you want to accelerate their reading growth. It is habit forming!

ow that she has thought through some ways of helping her students build reading stamina, Kemmery decides to begin an independent silent reading time by generating a list of guidelines with her students such as the one shown previously. She tells them that one important part of being a reader is being able to stay focused on what you are reading for several minutes. To help students understand the idea of *reading stamina*, she connects it with their own lives, stating, "Have you ever been playing outside and even though you got a little tired you kept playing?" Several students comment that they have, so she asks, "Why do you keep playing if you get tired? Turn, talk, and listen to what your neighbor has to say." After giving students time to talk with one another, she elicits comments from volunteers.

George comments, "Because it's fun and I just don't want to stop!"

Kemmery uses George's comment to make the connection to reading. "Exactly! And the same is true with reading! Sometimes you might get a little tired, but you enjoy the reading so much that you stay with it. Some people call this having *reading stamina*. It builds over time. Just like when playing a new game, you might decide to stop after five minutes. But the better you get at it, the longer you stay with it because you are having fun with it."

She concludes by stating, "We are going to continue developing your reading stamina during silent reading time by gradually increasing the time spent on silent reading. We'll start with ten minutes."

Reading Out Loud with Partners

What Is the Goal?

We want students to understand that there are purposes for reading to others. Sometimes the purpose involves performing or entertaining. At other times, the purpose is to share information with others.

Why Is the Goal Important?

Students sometimes have misunderstandings about what really happens during reading. We want them to understand that in real life, readers most often read to themselves. But there are times when people read aloud, such as when they want to share something they have discovered or read aloud a part in an oral performance. Talk with the class about people the students know who have a responsibility that includes reading aloud or sharing information. Create a list that includes teachers, baby-sitters, librarians, parents, actors, announcers, ministers, politicians, and so on. Talk about the importance of practice before performing and sharing aloud. Suggest that sometimes having a partner when a reader is practicing can be helpful.

While creating authentic purposes for the performance activities that require practice is important, study-buddy systems are another way to free you up to work with other students. Because the study buddies are there to keep each other focused and engaged, you can better focus on students that need your attention.

How Can You Evaluate Your Current Efforts in Meeting This Goal?

One way that you can evaluate your efforts to have students read to someone is to allow them time to prepare a text to read to one other person or a small group of students and listen to how they perform. If the purpose of the sharing is to entertain, for example, listen for how students use their voices to draw listeners in. Do they use intonation and expression to convey the author's intended meaning? Do they read at a pace that sounds like language people would use in their everyday talking with one another?

You can also have students evaluate their effort on reading with others by having them reflect on their performances. Using a three-point Likert scale with 1 being "I need to do better" and 5 being "I did very well," students can rate themselves on statements such as

I used my voice so that it sounded like real talk.

I read at the right pace so that everyone could understand what I was reading.

I looked like I enjoyed what I was reading.

Listeners could also evaluate each reader and give their evaluations to the performer for additional information about their performance.

What Can You Use to Make Progress in Meeting This Goal?

There are many ways to devise study-buddy systems, which allow students to read aloud for authentic purposes. One that we have used in the past that we like is called the *read around* (Opitz and Rasinski 2008). In this activity, students read their texts and identify something they think others would find interesting. They then practice reading this idea to themselves in preparation for reading it to a study buddy.

Certain books also lend themselves well to study-buddy reading. They are books that are formatted in such a way that they can be shared between readers even when the readers' achievement levels differ. One of the nice things about starting with poetry is you can easily transform it into duet reading by marking different lines or stanzas for different readers. You can mark the same poem to create some demanding parts and some less demanding parts for different students. You can also put poetry anthologies in the hands of partners, since most anthologies contain some easy and some difficult poems. (Figure 3–6 identifies other texts with formats conducive to partner reading.) Each of these ways of reading accelerates instruction by providing students with material that is more challenging yet readable because of the support system used to help them read the text. In reading these books, they are in contact with rich vocabulary that they would not be able to access without these supports. Likewise, reading with a buddy who is more adept is one way for a student who is less so to catch up. The less adept student gets to hear what reading can and should sound like and see what readers do when the need to problem-solve arises.

How Else Can You Use This Technique to Accelerate Instruction?

In study-buddy systems, you want to look both at how you can strengthen the interaction between the two partners and how you can continue to get more mileage from the activity you have introduced. Tightening up partner interaction and extending the exploration of the text will allow you to use other activities that have been shown to accelerate reading growth. For example, once you have introduced partners to the poetry club, you can build on and extend the use of poetry texts. Have each of your students create a poetry folder for use during independent reading time. When poems are introduced in the class, hand out hard copies that students can place in their folders. While the whole poems are good for independent and buddy reading practice, you can also develop independent word work activities using the poems. You can ask students to slip their poems in plastic protector sheets and put wipe-off markers in their folders. Working with partners or with you, they can search for and practice words, focusing on sound—symbol, structural, or meaning-based clues. They can mark up their poems and wipe them clean for another activity.

Another option is to give each student a paper grid on which the student can copy the words from the poem or a stanza from the poem, writing one word per box on the grid. The student can cut the boxes on the grid apart and again practice word games using the word cards. You can also place the words from the poem on a numbered list that students can place into their folders. Working with partners, they can practice words together by calling out numbers and identifying the words next to them or calling out words and identifying the numbers next to them. Any friendly, familiar poem can easily provide a lot of practice activities for individuals and partners working independently. These can include independent work with connected text and word work.

To strengthen the interactions of partners, you can also introduce other structured activities for use with partners. *Paired reading* (Topping 1989) is one of these activities, and it often includes a study buddy, who can help his or her partner using these procedures:

1. The reader chooses something to read and shares the selection with the study buddy.
2. The reader and study buddy begin by reading the text aloud in unison.
3. When the reader wants to read alone, he or she taps the study buddy on the shoulder and the study buddy stops reading aloud.
4. Either the reader or the study buddy can stop along the way to talk about what is being read.
5. If a word is mispronounced or not understood, the study buddy helps the reader to figure it out or tells the reader the word.

Kemmery decides to use poetry club as a way to have her students read to interested others. After first explaining how she chooses poems to read aloud, she provides students with several poetry anthologies and provides time for each to choose a poem he or she would like to read to a partner. Once students have selected their poems, she tells them to practice reading to themselves several times so that when they pair up with their partners, they will be able to easily read the poems aloud. After this practice, she has students read their poems to their poetry buddies. Each person also gets to tell why he or she selected the poem.

She meets with so much success using this strategy that she decides to try the read around during small-group reading time. She instructs each student to choose a sentence from a book he or she has been reading during independent silent reading time and to share it with others in the group, giving the title and author of the book, a brief synopsis, and why the sentence was selected to share with the group. She finds that not only are students in the groups interested in what their group members have to share but also their eyes are opened to texts they might want to read in the future that they previously had not been aware of.

Figure 3–6 Good Books for Study-Buddy Reading

Poetry Anthologies	Two readers can share one anthology, reading different poems to each other, allowing for reading at different levels.
Plays	Two readers can share one script, reading different parts to each other based on demands of the reading for each role.
Multilevel Texts	Many texts—especially informational texts—have text features written at different levels. For example, an alphabet book might have an explanatory line for each letter and then a more extended description for that topic. One reader can read the explanatory line and the other, the description.
Read-Together Books	Mary Ann Hoberman has five anthologies in the You Read to Me, I'll Read to You series. In them, short fairy tales, scary tales, fables, and Mother Goose rhymes have been formatted with colored lines that can be assigned to different readers as they practice the same story together.
We-Both-Read Books	Treasure Bay Publishers has a variety of fiction and nonfiction texts formatted to be read by parents and children. One page has more complex text and the next page has less demanding text. Readers at different levels can be paired and assigned the appropriate pages.
Cumulative Tales	The additive quality of cumulative tales makes them good books for partner reading. Each partner can read different parts. The reader who may need practice to internalize some of the vocabulary can read the repeated text whereas the other partner who might not need this repetition can read the new text that is added to the evolving cumulative text.
Repetitive Books	The repeating parts of these texts are good books for partner reading. The stronger reader can take the lead, focusing on the new, changing part of the book, and the other reader can focus on the repeating features.

Text Response Activities

What Is the Goal?

Students should understand that readers respond to the texts they read in many ways. Sometimes responses are oral, whereas other times they are written. Students should be comfortable with both oral and written response options.

Why Is the Goal Important?

Responding to texts is something readers do in their everyday lives as a way of showing their connection to the ideas they encounter in a text. Depending on the purpose for reading, responses can focus on factual information gleaned from the text or on the emotional reaction or feelings that the reader has about what he or she has read. It's important for students to understand that these are both valid types of responses and to be comfortable deciding which type of response they might want to create. Both types of responses show comprehension and can be used as catalysts for discussion.

Beyond the types of responses, students also need to see that responses can and do take on many forms—oral, written, visual displays, or any combination of these. Readers often choose the most germane format to use.

How Can You Evaluate Your Current Efforts in Meeting This Goal?

You can use students' written performances as one indicator of how well they are learning to respond to texts. For example, after you show students how to use two-column notes (see the numbered list in the next section), have them use the tool to respond to texts. Then evaluate how well they were able to use this type of response by looking at their two-column notes. Reviewing the class performance as a whole will help you see how well students are able to use this type of response and identify those who might need some additional help.

Likewise, after you show them how to question the author (see next section), you can listen to how students talk about the texts they are reading and the types of questions they ask about what the author included or excluded and why.

To help students develop an understanding of how to respond to text by pulling factual information from it, show them how to use two-column notes (Opitz and Schendel 2011). This tool helps students respond to text during and after reading and entails having students fold a piece of paper in half and make notes in each column. The left-hand column can be used for questions about the text the student is reading and the right-hand column can be used for recording corresponding answers discovered within the text.

To help students develop an understanding of how to make responses that center on how they feel about the text and what they are thinking about the text, show them how to use a strategy called *questioning the author* (Beck et al. 1997). With this comprehension strategy, the teacher uses questioning to lead students to evaluate an author's intent for writing a text and why the author included—or omitted—information. To do so, follow these teaching procedures:

1. Select a text that presents opportunities to consider an author's overall purpose, an author's choice of words, ideas supporting the author's purposes, or patterns found within the text.
2. Read the text carefully, placing sticky notes to indicate places in the text that will elicit discussion regarding the following:
   - what the author is trying to say; in other words, the overall purpose
   - what the choice of words does to help the purpose
   - what the author has left out and why
   - whether the author is clear in his or her presentation of ideas
   - how the author encourages the reader to connect to the text and make inferences
3. Introduce the general topic of the lesson.
4. Guide students through an interactive read-aloud, stopping at the predetermined places in the text and eliciting responses from students.
5. As a class, determine the author's overall message, and then ask students to think about how it applies in their own lives.

Visual displays are yet another way that readers respond to text, and you can show students how to create them. For example, you can show them the story mapper technique (Opitz and Schendel 2011), which involves using a graphic organizer to identify story elements such as character, setting, and conflict in text boxes. Students can use this map to prepare themselves for the text they will be reading and use it during reading. As they identify the information, they can write it in the corresponding box on the organizer. Students can also use their completed story mapper as a catalyst for discussion after reading the text.

But some students might be better off either drawing or finding pictures to visually represent different ideas within the text. Their final visual display might look something like a treasure map.

The adage that a picture is worth a thousand words explains why these visual representations are important. For some students, using visuals is the best way to show comprehension of what they have read. Enabling them to use visuals allows them this strength to show understanding that they cannot show in words. Consequently, rather than being viewed as poor comprehenders (who need more instruction when in fact they don't), they are seen as good comprehenders who need only instruction that focuses on ways to use words to respond to text. Acceleration then occurs because time is spent on teaching something they need to know.

Kemmery sees that her students are able to use writing to respond to texts and that they are fairly adept at responding in both factual and emotional ways. What she sees lacking is students' ability to use visual displays when responding to text. She decides to show students how to use pictures or symbols and explains the story mapper activity to them. Kemmery comments, "I am going to have you listen to this story three times. The first time I am going to read the entire story. The second time I am going to reread the story and show you how to create a visual story map using pictures rather than words to tell important parts of the story. Third, I am going to have you do a retelling of the story as I point to the pictures I have created on my visual display. Let's give it a try." After following this process, Kemmery asks students to try it on their own, saying, "I want you to choose any story that you find interesting. Read through the story the first time. Then, read it again and do your mapping. Third, partner up and share your visual story mapper with another person."

OUR CONCLUDING THOUGHTS

One of our goals in writing this book was to challenge the assumption that any one part of the instructional day can be enough to carry the burden for addressing the differences students bring to the classroom. If we are going to close the gap so that we move from reaching many with most to reaching every with all, we need to focus on that goal throughout the school day, throughout the school week, and throughout the school year. In this book, we have looked at ways to start that effort—to address acceleration by focusing on tightening whole groups, small groups, and independent instruction.

This is easier said than done. If it is to happen, then we need to challenge conventional wisdom. As Ed discovered (see Section 2), instructional acceleration rarely happens even when a teacher follows what is typically best practice. For example, on any given day, teachers usually have time set aside for whole-group interactive or shared reading experiences, but most teachers usually select an at- or above-level text to use with the class. When that text is set aside, unless that text has been positioned effectively with mediated instruction, it is accessible for the readers who are at and above grade level but not for those who are reading below grade level.

During the time set aside for small-group reading instruction, teachers may be more intentional about selecting an appropriate text for each group, but in most cases juggling multiple small groups means that instruction with any one group lasts about twenty minutes. Consequently, students spend more time doing independent reading and other literacy work, away from the teacher, instead of working with the teacher in small-group instruction. Independent work can be beneficial, but only if the independent work is designed so that students can continue to enhance their literacy understanding by engaging with at-level material.

Notice that in these typical literacy block practices, the readers in need of the most instruction often receive the least. Keep in mind what happens to those readers if the teacher doesn't differentiate texts during small-group instruction or the teacher does not provide accessible texts during independent reading time. It is quite easy to see how common classroom practices can actually expand the gap between striving readers and their classmates. The problem gets worse once the teacher moves back to a central text for content instruction. Then the class is back to where it started, working with a text that will be accessible for some but not all readers.

Unfortunately, many current initiatives to address this issue of accelerating the growth of all readers are falling short of closing the achievement gaps. Recall the aha moment we described in Section 2. At a workshop we were presenting that focused on differentiation through flexible grouping, a reading specialist confronted us during the morning break. We had commented that depending on the purpose of instruction, sometimes a teacher may need to weave in and out of large-group and small-group reading throughout the week, allowing some days for large-group reading and other days for small-group reading, especially if juggling both on the same day seems more daunting than doable. Our comment bothered the reading specialist, who was looking for affirmation about her school's recent effort to rearrange the literacy block to allow for thirty minutes of small-group guided reading with at-level texts every day. As she described the block, students were placed in leveled groups across classrooms. Students moved to other classrooms to work with others at the same levels as needed during this block of time.

While we applauded the effort to guarantee instruction with appropriate text for each child every day, we began to wonder about the burden that the thirty-minute block would have to carry to address the needs of all learners! Yes, thirty minutes with an appropriate text was better than zero minutes with an appropriate text, but we did have to ask what was going on during the rest of the school day. What was happening during the other six and a half hours available for instruction? Did the school staff really believe growth could be accelerated by attending to that goal for only thirty minutes a day? Clearly, if instruction is critical, it matters throughout the day and the week. Accelerating the growth of all learners cannot be consigned to a thirty-minute block, despite what we have observed: the increasing presence of differentiation and intervention blocks in many schools. If we start looking for ways to accelerate the growth of all learners, we need to look beyond relegating the burden for intervention to a small part of the school day or school week.

You can see evidence of this in a posting on the Wisconsin State Reading Association hotline. It surfaced the desperation of one reading specialist trying to meet the request of her administrators: "Our district wants to improve instructional support and student learning in the areas of word learning, comprehension, decoding and fluency. Please contact me about programs that classroom teachers have implemented in your schools, specifically programs that would fit into a 30-minute intervention block 3 times per week." Again, if we are going to accelerate the growth of all readers in all these areas, there is probably a slim likelihood of that happening when intervention is left to three thirty-minute periods a week. That's not to say that that time would not be valuable for certain learners, but it does continue to raise this question: What is happening during the other parts of the school day and school week?

Unfortunately, current models conceptualized within the response-to-intervention standard protocol frameworks may be exacerbating the problems. You've seen the pyramids. Some RTI models actually start with the assumption that tier one instruction, which is usually regular classroom instruction, should reach 80 to 85 percent of learners. Any model that starts with an assumption that it is acceptable to fail to reach one out of every six learners and instead let additional levels of intervention reach them shifts the burden to one part of the school day instead of placing the burden on all parts of the school day. Tier one instruction virtually guarantees the best we can do is reach many with most, but not attempt to reach every with all.

If instruction matters, then educators must think about acceleration throughout the day. In this book we have examined fifteen classroom catalysts, but we fully acknowledge that any one in and of itself will not increase the growth of all learners. The ideas in this book and the similar ideas we referred to need to be used collectively and in a pervasive manner. Acceleration, like differentiation, is more a way of thinking about instruction. To benefit all learners, acceleration must be a prioritized outcome and an intentional way of operating with instruction throughout the day in whole groups, small groups, and independent activities. We remain steadfast in our belief that expert teachers can and do work toward this most important outcome every day. We hope that the contents of this book will help you in your quest to achieve accelerated growth for all learners. Imagine . . . finally reaching every reader with all that he or she needs.

APPENDICES

Grouping-Without-Tracking Lesson Plan

Objective: _____

Text	
Front-loading (Before Reading) **Large Groups**	
Reading and Responding (During Reading) **Small Groups**	
Extending (After Reading) **Large Groups**	

Jigsaw Lesson Plan

Objective: _____

Text Sections to be read by different teams or groups of students	_____ 1: _____ 2: _____ 3: _____ 4: _____
Front-loading (Before Reading) **Large Groups**	
Reading and Responding (During Reading) **Small Groups**	
Extending (After Reading) **Large Groups**	

Connected Literature Circles Lesson Plan

Objective: _____

Texts	1. 2. 3. 4.
Frontloading (Before Reading) **Large Groups**	
Reading and Responding (During Reading) **Small Groups**	
Extending (After Reading) **Large Groups**	

REFERENCES

Allington, Richard L. 1983. "The Reading Instruction Provided Readers of Differing Reading Abilities." *The Elementary School Journal* 83 (5): 548–59.

———. 2008. "If They Don't Read Much . . . 30 Years Later." In *Reading More, Reading Better*, ed. Elfrieda Heibert, 30–54. New York: Guilford.

Allington, Richard L., and Patricia M. Cunningham. 2007. *Schools That Work: Where All Children Read and Write*. Boston: Pearson/Allyn and Bacon.

Allington, Richard L., and Peter H. Johnston. 2002. *Reading to Learn: Lessons from Exemplary Fourth-Grade Classrooms*. New York: Guilford.

Alvermann, Donna. 1984. "Teaching the Process of Inferring Through a Listening Guide." *Reading Horizons* 24 (4): 243–48.

Anderson, Richard. 1996. "Research Foundations to Support Wide Reading." In *Promoting Reading in Developing Countries*, ed. Vincent Greaney, 55–77. Newark, DE: International Reading Association.

Aronson, Elliot. 1978. *The Jigsaw Classroom*. Beverly Hills, CA: Sage.

Bacon, Arthur, and Henry Bacon. 2008. *I Hate Reading: How to Get Through 20 Minutes of Reading a Day Without Really Reading*. Fort Atkinson, WI: Upstart Books.

Beck, Isabel L., Margaret G. McKeown, Rebecca L. Hamilton, and Linda Kucan. 1997. *Questioning the Author: An Approach for Enhancing Student Engagement with Text*. Newark, DE: International Reading Association.

Betts, Emmet. 1946. *Foundations of Reading Instruction*. New York: American Book Company.

Bomer, Randy. 1998. "Transactional Heat and Light: More Explicit Literacy Learning." *Language Arts* 76 (1): 11–18.

Boushey, Gail, and Joan Moser. 2014. *The Daily Five*. 2d ed. Portland, ME: Stenhouse.

Brophy, Jere. 1987. "Synthesis of Research on Strategies for Motivating Students to Learn." *Educational Leadership* 45 (2): 40–48.

Caldwell, JoAnne, and Michael P. Ford. 2002. *Where Have All the Bluebirds Gone?* Portsmouth, NH: Heinemann.

Cohen, Elisabeth G. 1994. *Designing Groupwork: Strategies for the Heterogeneous Classroom.* New York: Teachers College Press.

Cooper, Elisha. 2013. *Train.* New York: Scholastic.

Correnti, Richard. 2006. "Using Daily Teacher Logs to Demonstrate Professional Development Effects on Literacy Instruction." Paper presented at the annual meeting of the American Educational Research Association, San Francisco, April 10.

Cuyler, Margery. 2009. *Bullies Never Win.* New York: Simon and Schuster.

DeHaven, Edna. 1989. *Teaching and Learning the Language Arts.* 3rd ed. New York: Scott Foresman.

Dewitz, Peter, Jennifer Jones, and Susan Leahy. 2009. "Comprehension Strategy Instruction in Core Reading Programs." *Reading Research Quarterly* 44 (2): 102–26.

Dorn, Linda J., and Carla Soffos. 2011. *Interventions That Work: A Comprehensive Intervention Model for Preventing Reading Failure in Grades K–3.* Boston: Pearson.

Ford, Michael P. 2005. "Improving Classroom Participation by Engaging and Honoring All Voices in Large and Small Groups." *Colorado Reading Council Journal* 16: 13–17.

Ford, Michael P., and Michael F. Opitz. 2002. "Using Centers to Engage Children During Guided Reading Time: Intensifying Learning Experiences Away from the Teacher." *The Reading Teacher* 55 (8): 710–17.

———. 2010. "From Many and Most to Every and All: Research-Based Strategies for Moving All Readers Forward." *Illinois State Reading Journal* 38: 3–13.

Frey, Nancy, Douglas Fisher, and Sandi Everlove. 2009. *Productive Group Work: How to Engage Students, Build Teamwork, and Promote Understanding.* Alexandria, VA: ASCD.

Gamse, Beth C., Robin Tepper Jacob, Megan Horst, Beth Boulay, and Fatih Unlu. 2008. *Reading First Impact Study Final Report.* NCEE 2009-4038. Washington, DC: National Center for Education Evaluation and Regional Assistance.

Glasswell, Kath, and Michael Ford. 2011. "Let's Start Leveling About Leveling." *Language Arts* 88 (3): 208–16.

Greydanus, Rose. 1983. *Changing Seasons.* Now I Know series. Mahwah, NJ: Troll.

Guthrie, John, Allan Wigfield, Jamie Metsala, and Kathleen Cox. 1999. "Motivational and Cognitive Predictors of Text Comprehension and Reading Amount." *Scientific Studies of Reading* 3: 231–56.

International Reading Association (IRA). 2012. *Literacy Implementation Guidance for ELA Common Core State Standards.* Newark, DE: International Reading Association.

Irvine, Patricia D., and Joanne Larson. 2007. "Literacy Packages in Practice: Constructing Academic Disadvantage." In *Literacy as Snake Oil: Beyond the Quick Fix*, 2d ed., ed. Joanne Larson, 49–71. New York: Lang.

Kelly, Sean, and Julianne Turner. 2009. "Rethinking the Effects of Classroom Activity Structure on the Engagement of Low-Achieving Students." *The Teachers College Record* 111 (7): 1665–92.

Krashen, Stephen D. 1993. *The Power of Reading: Insights from the Research.* Englewood, CO: Libraries Unlimited.

Lesesne, Teri S. 2010. *Reading Ladders: Leading Students from Where They Are to Where We'd Like Them to Be.* Portsmouth, NH: Heinemann.

Levesque, Jeri. 1989. "ELVES: A Read-Aloud Strategy to Develop Listening Comprehension." *The Reading Teacher* 43 (1): 93–94.

Linehart, Gaea, Naomi Zigmond, and William Cooley. 1981. "Reading Instruction and Its Effects." *American Educational Research Journal* 18: 343–61.

McCarthy, Meghan. 2007. *Strong Man: The Story of Charles Atlas*. New York: Alfred A. Knopf.

McRae, Angela, and John T. Guthrie. 2008. "Promoting Reasons for Reading: Teacher Practices That Impact Motivation." In *Reading More, Reading Better*, ed. Elfrieda Heibert, 55–77. New York: Guilford.

National Governors Association (NGA) Center for Best Practices and Council of Chief State School Officers (CCSSO). 2010. *Common Core State Standards for English Language Arts and Literacy in History/Social Studies, Science, and Technical Subjects*. Washington, DC: NGA Center for Best Practices and CCSSO. Available at www.corestandards.org/ELA-Literacy.

Oczkus, Lori D. 2004. *Super 6 Comprehension Strategies: 35 Lessons and More for Reading Success*. Norwood, MA: Christopher-Gordon.

Opitz, Michael F., and Michael P. Ford. 2001. *Reaching Readers: Flexible and Innovative Strategies for Guided Reading*. Portsmouth, NH: Heinemann.

———. 2008. *Do-able Differentiation: Varying Groups, Texts, and Supports to Reach Readers*. Portsmouth, NH: Heinemann.

Opitz, Michael F., Michael P. Ford, with Matthew Zbaracki. 2006. *Books and Beyond: New Ways to Reach Readers*. Portsmouth, NH: Heinemann.

Opitz, Michael, and Timothy Rasinski. 2008. *Good-Bye Round Robin: 25 Effective Oral Reading Strategies*. Rev. ed. Portsmouth, NH: Heinemann.

Opitz, Michael, and Roland Schendel. 2011. *25 Essential Language Arts Strategies to Help Striving Readers Succeed*. New York: Scholastic.

Opitz, Michael, and Matthew Zbaracki. 2004. *Listen Hear! 25 Effective Listening Comprehension Strategies*. Portsmouth, NH: Heinemann.

Paratore, Jeanne. 1990. "Classroom Contexts for Literacy Training: Flexible Grouping." Paper presented at the Wisconsin State Reading Association, Eau Claire, WI, October 6.

Patterson, James. 2014. Quote sent from his Twitter account (@JP_Books), January 9. Available at https://twitter.com/JP_Books/status/4213448112248.

Pearson, P. David. 2009. "Reading Policy in America: A Checkered History, an Uneasy Present, and an Uncertain Future." Paper presented at the Wisconsin State Reading Association, Milwaukee, WI, February 5.

Pearson, P. David, and Margaret C. Gallagher. 1983. "The Gradual Release of Responsibility Model of Instruction." *Contemporary Educational Psychology* 8: 112–23.

Pressley, Michael, Richard Allington, Ruth Wharton-McDonald, Cathy Collins Block, and Lesley Mandel Morrow. 2001. *Learning to Read: Lessons Learned from Exemplary Classrooms*. New York: Guilford.

Reis, Sally M. 2009. *Joyful Reading: Differentiation and Enrichment for Successful Literacy Learning, Grades K–8*. San Francisco: Jossey-Bass.

Reis, Sally M., D. Betsy McCoach, Catherine A. Little, Lisa M. Muller, and R. Burcu Kaniskan. 2011. "The Effects of Differentiated Instruction and Enrichment Pedagogy on Reading Achievement in Five Elementary Schools." *American Educational Research Journal* 48 (2): 462–501.

Reutzel, D. Ray, and Paul M. Hollingsworth. 1991. "Investigating Topic-Related Attitude: Effect on Reading and Remembering Text." *Journal of Educational Research* 84 (6): 334–44.

Routman, Regie. 2003. *Reading Essentials*. Portsmouth, NH: Heinemann.

Rowan, Brian, Richard Correnti, Robert J. Miller, and Eric M. Camburn. 2009. *School Improvement by Design: Lessons from a Study of Comprehensive School Reform Programs*. Philadelphia: Consortium for Policy Research in Education.

Rubin, Dorothy. 2000. *Teaching Elementary Language Arts*. 6th ed. New York: Allyn and Bacon.

Schmoker, Mike. 2010. "When Pedagogic Fads Trump Priorities." *Education Week* 30 (5): 22–23.

Shannon, Patrick. 2013. "Re-reading Poverty: Reorienting Educational Policy." In *Whose Knowledge Counts in Government Literacy Policies? Why Expertise Matters*, ed. Kenneth S. Goodman, Robert C. Calfee, and Yetta M. Goodman, 37–46. New York: Routledge.

Sibberson, Franki. 2013. "A Life Without Reading." Blog post. July 22. http://nerdybookclub .wordpress.com/2013/07/22/a-life-without-reading-by-franki-sibberson/.

Stahl, Steven A., and Kathleen M. Heubach. 2005. "Fluency-Oriented Reading Instruction." *Journal of Literacy Research* 37 (1): 25–60.

Stanovich, Keith E. 1986. "Matthew Effects in Reading: Some Consequences of Individual Differences in the Acquisition of Literacy." *Reading Research Quarterly* 21 (4): 360–407.

Stuhlman, Megan W., and Robert C. Pianta. 2009. "Profiles of Educational Quality in First Grade." *The Elementary School Journal* 109 (4): 323–42.

Tatum, Alfred W. 2009. *Reading for Their Life: (Re)building the Textual Lineages of African American Adolescent Males*. Portsmouth, NH: Heinemann.

Taylor, Barbara M., P. David Pearson, Kathleen F. Clark, and Sharon Walpole. 1999. "Effective Schools/Accomplished Teachers." *The Reading Teacher* 53 (2): 156–59.

Tomlinson, Carol A. 1999. *The Differentiated Classroom: Responding to the Needs of All Learners*. Alexandria, VA: ASCD.

Topping, Keith. 1989. "Peer Tutoring and Paired Reading: Combining Two Powerful Techniques." *The Reading Teacher* 42 (7): 488–94.

Veatch, Jeanette. 1968. *How to Teach Reading with Children's Books*. New York: R. C. Owen.

Wlodkowski, Raymond J., and Margery B. Ginsberg. 1995. "A Framework for Culturally Responsive Teaching." *Educational Leadership* 53 (1): 17–21.

Youngs, Suzette. 2012. "Understanding History Through the Visual Images in Historical Fiction." *Language Arts* 89 (6): 379–95.